**Volume 02
Issue 01
March 2007**

The Senses & Society

BERG

AIMS AND SCOPE

A heightened interest in the role of the senses in culture and society is sweeping the human sciences, supplanting older paradigms and challenging conventional theories of representation.

This pioneering journal provides a crucial forum for the exploration of this vital new area of inquiry. It brings together groundbreaking work in the humanities and social sciences and incorporates cutting-edge developments in art, design, and architecture. Every volume contains something for and about each of the senses, both singly and in all sorts of novel configurations.

Sensation is fundamental to our experience of the world. Shaped by culture, gender, and class, the senses mediate between mind and body, idea and object, self and environment. The senses are increasingly extended beyond the body through technology, and catered to by designers and marketers, yet persistently elude all efforts to capture and control them. Artists now experiment with the senses in bold new ways, disrupting conventional canons of aesthetics.

- How is perception shaped by cultures and technologies?
- In what ways are the senses sites for the production and practice of ideologies of gender, class, and race?
- How many senses are there to "aesthetics"?
- What are the social implications of the increasing commercialization of sensation?
- How might a focus on the cultural life of the senses yield new insights into processes of cognition and emotion?

The Senses & Society aims to:

- Explore the intersection between culture and the senses
- Promote research on the politics of perception and the aesthetics of everyday life
- Address architectural, marketing, and design initiatives in relation to the senses
- Publish reviews of books and multi-sensory exhibitions throughout the world
- Publish special issues concentrating on particular themes relating to the senses

To submit an article, please write to Michael Bull at:

The Senses and Society
Department of Media & Film Studies
University of Sussex
Brighton
Sussex
BN1 9QQ
UK

email:
senses@sussex.ac.uk or
m.bull@sussex.ac.uk

Books for review should be sent to David Howes at:

The Senses and Society
Department of Sociology and Anthropology
Concordia University
1455 de Maisonneuve Boulevard West
Montreal, Quebec
H3G 1M8
CANADA

email:
senses@alcor.concordia.ca
howesd@alcor.concordia.ca

Comments and suggestions regarding Sensory Design reviews should be addressed to Joy Monice Malnar

email:
malnar@uiuc.edu

Comments and suggestions regarding multisensory exhibition and conference reviews should be addressed to Jim Drobnick

email:
jdrobnick@faculty.ocad.ca

©2007 Berg. All rights reserved.
No part of this publication may be reproduced or utilized in any form or by any means, electronic or mechanical, including photocopying and recording, or by any information storage or retrieval system, without permission in writing from the publisher.

ISSN (print): 1745-8927
ISSN (online): 1745-8935

The Senses and Society is indexed by:
AIO – Anthropological Index Online (Royal Anthropological Library);
CSA: Sociological Abstracts; Baywood's Abstracts in Anthropology;
CSA: ARTbibliographies Modern; CSA: British Humanities Index; and
CSA: DAAI – Design and Applied Arts Index

Berg Publishers is a member of CrossRef

SUBSCRIPTION INFORMATION

Three issues per volume.

One volume per annum.

2007: Volume 2

ONLINE
www.bergpublishers.com

BY MAIL
Berg Publishers
C/o Customer Services
Turpin Distribution
Pegasus Drive
Stratton Business Park
Biggleswade
Bedfordshire SG18 8TQ
UK

BY FAX
+44 (0)1767 601640

BY TELEPHONE
+44 (0)1767 604951

BY EMAIL
custserv@turpin-distribution.com

INQUIRIES
Kathryn Earle, Managing Editor
email: kearle@bergpublishers.com

Production: Ian Critchley, email: icritchley@bergpublishers.com

Advertising and subscriptions:
Veruschka Selbach,
email: vselbach@bergpublishers.com

SUBSCRIPTION RATES

Print

Institutional: (1 year) $300/£165;
(2 year) $480/£264

Individual: (1 year) $70/£40*; (2 year) $112/£64*

Online only

Institutional and individual: (1 year) $240, £130; (2 year) $384, £208

*This price is available only to personal subscribers and must be prepaid by personal cheque or credit card

Free online subscription for institutional subscribers

Full color images available online

Access your electronic subscription through www.ingenta.com

REPRINTS FOR MAILING

Copies of individual articles may be obtained from the publishers at the appropriate fees.
Write to

Berg Publishers
1st Floor, Angel Court
81 St Clements Street
Oxford OX4 1AW
UK

Founding Editors

Michael Bull and David Howes

EDITORIAL BOARD

Managing Editor

Michael Bull, University of Sussex, UK

Editors

Paul Gilroy, London School of Economics, UK

David Howes, Concordia University, Canada

Douglas Kahn, University of California, Davis, USA

Sensory Design Editor

Joy Monice Malnar, University of Illinois, Urbana-Champaign

Book Reviews Editor

David Howes, Concordia University

Exhibition and Conference Reviews Editor

Jim Drobnick, Ontario College of Art and Design, Toronto, Canada

ADVISORY BOARD

Alison Clarke, *University of Vienna, Austria*

Steven Connor, *University of London, UK*

Alain Corbin, *Université de Paris I, La Sorbonne, France*

Ruth Finnegan, *Open University, UK*

Jukka Gronow, *University of Uppsala, Sweden*

Peter Charles Hoffer, *University of Georgia, USA*

Caroline Jones, *Massachusetts Institute of Technology, USA*

Barbara Kirshenblatt-Gimblett, *New York University, USA*

Margaret Morse, *University of California at Santa Cruz, USA*

Ruth Phillips, *Carleton University, Canada*

Leigh Schmidt, *Princeton University, USA*

Mark Smith, *University of South Carolina, USA*

Jonathan Sterne, *McGill University, Canada*

Paul Stoller, *West Chester University, USA*

Michael Syrotinski, *University of Aberdeen, UK*

Nigel Thrift, *University of Warwick, UK*

Fran Tonkiss, *London School of Economics, UK*

Typeset by JS Typesetting Ltd, Porthcawl, Mid Glamorgan
Printed in the UK

The Senses & Society

**Volume 02
Issue 01
March 2007**

Contents

Articles

5   **The Experience of Color**
    David MacDougall

27 **Seeing Isn't Believing: Blindness, Race, and Cultural Literacy**
    Elaine Gerber

41 **Regimes of Vision and Products of Color**
    Charlene Elliott

59 **Sensing Cittàslow: Slow Living and the Constitution of the Sensory City**
    Sarah Pink

Sensory Design

81 **Les Cols Restaurant: A Sensual Feast**
    Elias Vavaroutsos

87 **Midwest Skyspace**
    Frank Vodvarka

93 **IIT Muffles the L: The McCormick-Tribune Campus Center**
    Joy Monice Malnar

Book Reviews

101 **The Senses and Aesthetics from a Scandinavian Perspective:
    Per Bäckström and Troels Degn Johansson (eds.),
    *Sense and Senses in Aesthetics***
        Reviewed by Larry Shiner

105 **A Sense of History: Robert Jütte, *A History of the Senses:
    From Antiquity to Cyberspace***
        Reviewed by Mark M. Smith

109 **On the Varieties of Experience: Martin Jay, *Songs of Experience: Modern American and European Variations on a Universal Theme***
Reviewed by C. Jason Throop

Exhibition Reviews

117 **Sonambiente Berlin 2006: Festivale für hören und sehen**
Reviewed by Rosemary Heather

123 **Arsenal: Artists Exploring the Potential of Sound as a Weapon**
Reviewed by Francis Summers

The Experience of Color

David MacDougall

David MacDougall is a professorial fellow at the Australian National University's Centre for Cross-Cultural Research, an ethnographic filmmaker and the author of *Transcultural Cinema* and *The Corporeal Image: Film, Ethnography, and the Senses*. His present research is on schools and other institutions for children in India.
david.macdougall@anu.edu.au.

ABSTRACT Color serves a variety of purposes in society from identifying groups to conveying symbolic meanings to providing aesthetic pleasure. More subtle effects of color can be found in the environments that human communities construct around themselves. At Doon School, an elite boys' boarding school in northern India, color is intimately associated with the students' activities, social relationships and sensory experiences. It defines their status and shapes their everyday lives. The uses of color at the school are consistent with a wider social aesthetic emphasizing restraint, logical thought and the training and presentation of the body. Many of these values can be seen to have their origins in the school's colonial history and postcolonial aspirations.

KEYWORDS: color, senses, visual anthropology, aesthetics, schools, India

Color is but one of several aspects of vision, and only one of the many strands that make up our perception of the social and material world. It nevertheless plays an important part in the aesthetics of everyday life. Here I mean not the beauty-aesthetics of fine art or Kantian philosophy but something closer to the classical Greek concept of *aisthesis*, or sense experience, and what A.G. Baumgarten meant when he introduced the term into philosophy in the eighteenth century as "the science of sensory cognition." Aesthetics from this perspective has less to do with artistic expression and the exercise of taste than with the more mundane and pervasive forms of sensory patterning to be found in society, and the ways in which human beings experience and respond to them. It may even denote a particular set of attitudes toward how to live one's life – in Foucault's phrase, an "aesthetics of existence."

One place in which to study the social aesthetics of color is in the highly controlled environment of schools, where colors frequently become important signifiers. In many schools color is used for coding and identification, as it is by political parties, religious groups and sporting teams. These uses may or may not reflect national or cultural associations, such as the colors used in flags or linked to religions. In India, for example, colors carry culturally specific meanings that have both a political and religious significance: white being associated with mourning, purity and abstinence; green with Islam; blue with Brahmanism; and saffron with Hinduism – or latterly, Hindutva religiosity.

There are other uses to be considered. Schools use colors to focus the emotions of students and to set themselves apart from other schools. A pair of colors is often chosen because the number of available possibilities is thereby greatly increased. Students may not in fact identify with either color when it is used by itself but only when it is combined with the other. It is this binary that becomes meaningful, as in Eisenstein's theory of cinematic montage, where it is the juxtaposition of two shots that generates the meaning. If either color were paired off with a different color it would take on quite different associations. This principle applies to the co-presence of colors generally, allowing them to become closely associated in some contexts but used in opposition in others.

This is color-coding at a very rudimentary level, even though such uses may have powerful psychological effects. Equally important, however, are the less obvious effects of color, involving deeper cultural resonances, the effects of certain dominant colors, and the inclusion of color itself in a broader range of sensory experiences. Some individuals are known to experience synesthetic associations between sounds, physical shapes and specific colors. It is therefore not unlikely that the reverse is true: that for some people colors may correspond to certain qualities of sound, such as its timbre, or to certain physical forms, or even to certain textures and odors. In any case, colors do not exist in isolation but in relation to objects, events and other colors – and, sometimes, in relation to the absence of color. Color is a property of objects – or, more accurately, an effect of light. Objects project their other qualities into the colors with which they are clothed. Color only becomes "color" in the abstract when one begins to see it as a quality cutting across different contexts and binding together different objects. Colors may possess properties that have a direct impact on our bodily responses, but our sensing of color also takes place within the context of our emotions and social relationships. Colors rarely possess only a single symbolic value: they are multivalent, appearing in different circumstances and creating correspondingly complex and ambiguous feelings in those who experience them. How we respond to color is thus intimately linked to our activities, our language, our cultural associations and the events in our lives.

Blue, Gray and the Skin

Doon School, in northern India, is an elite boys' boarding school renowned for the greenness of its campus, the Chandbagh Estate. Until 1933 this formed the grounds of the Forest Research Institute and College. The students of the school inherited an extraordinary botanical garden of some seventy acres containing several hundred species of trees as well as beds filled with flowers and shrubs. Greenness was the dominant impression I had of the school when I first visited it in 1996. This occurred during a mid-term break when the students were away on excursions. I remember seeing massive trees of all kinds and at the heart of the school a broad green playing field bordered by dormitories and other buildings. When I returned to the school the following April I began to see flickerings of blue through the foliage. This was the blue of the students' games uniforms, which consisted of shorts of a deep blue color and shirts with a pattern of blue and gray panels. Inescapable green was now succeeded by inescapable blue.

It was the shirt of the games uniform that produced one of the more memorable statements of the school's first headmaster, A.E. Foot. Addressing the assembled boys in 1936, he said "You can think of yourselves as a pack of cards all with the same pattern of blue and gray on your backs; on the other side is each boy's special character." Foot was fond of such metaphors and their implications. In referring to the school's two official colors he was underlining several important distinctions. His use of the metaphor of the back and the front may be taken in two senses. His main point is to draw a line between the school as an institution and as a collection of living human beings. In the image of the pack of cards he suggests the

David MacDougall

Figure 1
The Doon School Games Uniform.

potential for conflict between individuality and uniformity, as though to stress the boys' need to guard their special qualities.[1] At the same time, he does not deny the value of seeing oneself as a member of a social unit. The student thus bears a dual relation to the school, on the one hand as an autonomous personality, on the other as a responsible citizen. This duality is reinforced by the way in which the design of the games shirt both unifies and effectively splits the boy down the middle. More concretely, a distinction may be drawn between the actual cloth of the uniforms and the boys' faces and bodies, between, that is, inert matter and flesh, the incorporeal and corporeal – and, one might add, between manufactured goods produced by human beings and human beings themselves. There is one thing more. In relating the school colors to positive and negative (or neutral) qualities Foot may be alluding to the difference between color and non-color, for according to some definitions gray is not a color at all but an absence of color.[2] This has implications for how the school handles color generally and the selective use of color and non-color throughout the school.[3]

One further consideration is implicit in Foot's statement. Blue and gray both stand in direct opposition to the varieties of skin color of north Indians. The difference would be less pronounced if the Doon School uniforms included yellow or red, often considered "warm" colors in comparison to blue.[4] And indeed, among the *ganas* – the Hindu categories of human behavior and natural phenomena (literally, "strings" or "strands") – the *rajas gana*, or red, is the *gana* of passion and energy. Could blue and gray, a "cool" color and a non-color, have been chosen to make precisely this contrast with the warmer color of the boys' skins? If boys were blue, would their uniforms have been orange or pink? Or is the contrast merely a fortuitous underpinning of Foot's main point? This is not an entirely idle matter, for if one of the uses of uniforms and color is to contain and control the body, then in this context blue becomes the color of maximum control.

Consciousness of the skin, and skin color in particular, are matters of some importance and complexity in Indian society, a fact that must at some level influence the attitudes of students and staff at the school. Considerable attention is paid to the perfection of the skin. The smoothness, glow and well-being of the skin is considered a significant part of looking attractive. I noticed that even preadolescent boys at Doon School spent a large amount of time on grooming. For many of them this included, along with assiduously brushing their teeth and combing their hair, rubbing their skin with creams and oils several times a day. In India these practices are not confined to the middle class but are found at all levels of society. Allied to this, the lightness or darkness of the skin is part of the subtext of Indian attitudes toward caste. There is no strict correlation between skin color and caste, but there is often assumed to be a connection. This is complicated by the fact that people from the south are generally darker than people from the north, regardless of caste. In the matrimonial advertisements in Indian newspapers, young women are often described as "fair," the currently most common term for light skin color. (A few years ago, "wheatish" was the popular term.) Although I never heard skin color discussed openly at Doon, it is reasonable to assume that the color of the skin is an element in the complex of body and uniform that defines boys individually and arrayed in groups.

Green, as I have already noted, is the dominant color of the school's surroundings, the color of foliage, playing fields and even the local parrots. It is so omnipresent as to form an unconscious background to all school activities. It is the color of nature, not of human intervention, and indeed appears to stand in opposition to the field of human order, which is represented by the school's buildings and walls. Against the towering trees, the students, dressed in blue and gray, seem small units of another order when massed together in sports or school rituals. As if to counter the green, the school's buildings are of warmer colors, some of them, including the original Forest Research Institute building, of red brick. A number of other brick buildings are painted red, as if to intensify this color.[5] Most buildings have red roofs. Low walls bordering the pathways are painted red, as are the arches of a viaduct that once brought water to the estate. The school's outdoor theater, the Rose Bowl, is reddish in color as well as in name. Green and red thus constitute a pair of opposites at the school, but one that seems confined to the physical setting.

It is also apparent that green stands in contrast to the three elements of the triad: blue-gray-skin color. One would therefore expect

Figure 2
The Main Building.

a general avoidance of green in most aspects of the school's social life. However, this proves not to be the case. The athletics singlets worn by the students of Jaipur House, and used in inter-house competitions, are in fact dark green. At first sight, this could be put down to the simple need to color-code the five main residential houses of the school, although the school's general inclination seems to be toward blue in its uniforms. (When a fifth house, Oberoi House, was added to the original four, the color chosen for its singlet was a kind of turquoise or peacock blue – a shade sufficiently different to distinguish it from the dark blue of Hyderabad House.) But if the green of the Jaipur House singlets is an exception, it is an odd one, since other colors were available when the choice was made. That it is not an exception is further supported by the fact that in the school's dormitories the bedcovers are either green or blue. In fact, blue and green seem to be closely allied here, as they are in the color spectrum. We may posit that this is so because they serve equally well to provide a contrast to human life. Thus green is treated in two distinct ways depending on its context. In the broader sphere of the built environment, such as the exteriors of buildings, it is avoided. In more intimate circumstances, such as the boys' sleeping arrangements or clothing seen next to their skin, it becomes acceptable, and perhaps even a desirable counterpoint.

Color and Identity

The importance of color at Doon, and its controlled use in clothing, may be cause for some puzzlement, particularly at a school with a strong if sometimes paradoxical ethic of individual worth. However, this very ethic may be one of the reasons behind it. The complete absence of variegated color, in contrast to the clothes worn by students at home, makes the presence of color, and the selective use of colors particularly striking.

Terence Turner has argued that external signs of social identity, such as color, may be more important in non-exchange societies than in societies in which material exchange is highly developed:

> Societies in which social identity is not constituted primarily through the exchange of goods (valuables, gifts, or commodities) nevertheless depend on the public circulation of symbolic tokens of valued aspects of personal identity, such as marks of status, appropriate role performance, and the values associated with them. In the absence of concrete objects that might serve as embodiments of such values or tokens of status, a society may make use of other modes of circulation that do not rely on the exchange of objects. … [One] mode of circulation is through visual display. In the case of circulating tokens of personal identity and value, such display typically involves specialized forms of bodily appearance. (1995: 147)

An elite boarding school such as Doon could be considered a non-exchange society. Students are there to study and build up knowledge and merit, not commodities. The commodities, it is hoped, will come later, assured by a Doon education. Tokens of wealth are few, and a boy from a very modest background may sleep next to a boy from one of the richest families in the country. There would be little visibly to distinguish them. Boys in their first year are forbidden to wear watches, partly to discourage a show of wealth. Pocket money is limited and doled out by means of coupons from a "Boys' Bank." One of the few areas in which boys can display wealth is in the wearing of expensive track shoes, but this is a fairly recent phenomenon.

Turner gives as an illustration of his argument the highly coded use of color in body painting among the Kayapo of the Amazon basin. At Doon, variations in color and uniforms, as extensions of the body, also become important indicators of status and affiliation. Variations in uniform, some obvious, some subtle, indicate one's house, one's seniority and one's personal achievements. Doon's system of dressing its boys is thus perhaps no less elaborate than the painting of Kayapo bodies. There are different uniforms for different occasions in which both color and the lack of color carry significance. The use of color and its absence become part of the students' everyday experience at the school.

After spending several weeks at Doon School my overall impression was not so much one of varied uses of color as of monochromes. Where colors are evident they tend to appear in isolation, or in association with gray. They stand out in their simplicity. This creates a kind of stripping-down of sensory experience in school life. It is in many ways restful in comparison to the chaotic medley of color on the streets beyond the gates. Monochrome provides an ordered background to life and a suppression of difference but also, paradoxically, a background against which individual differences – in faces, bodily appearance and manner – may stand out all the more strongly. In the long-standing debate about school uniforms this difference of emphasis is a recurrent theme. Uniforms, it is argued by some, encourage conformity and suppress individuality; they are inherently authoritarian and undemocratic. Others argue, to the contrary, that uniforms are egalitarian. They iron out differences of wealth and provide a common ground against which the merits of the individual can shine. This is the view implicit in A.E. Foot's pack-of-cards metaphor.

Doon School's monochromes are evident in its uniforms, its interior spaces and its natural setting. Here green is the monochrome of nature, the environment in which social life goes on. The school uniforms are studies in monochrome. They vary throughout the day, the changes determined by school activities, the seniority of the boys wearing them and the seasons. Changes in activities establish a repetitive temporal sequence. A typical day involves five changes of uniform, or possibly even more if a boy is being punished.[6] Upon waking, the boys go immediately for PT (physical training), a set of exercises on the playing field supervised by staff members and other students. For this activity they change from their nightwear into a white singlet, dark blue shorts and white gym shoes with white socks. (In winter they may be allowed a white pullover or a gray and blue tracksuit.) After PT they change into their classroom uniform. In winter this is a gray woolen suit, white shirt, sometimes

Figure 3
The Winter Classroom Uniform.

a school tie (gray with narrow blue stripes), gray school stockings and black shoes. Except on formal occasions, a gray pullover may be substituted for the suit jacket and a blue shirt for the white one. Junior boys are allowed to wear gray shorts instead of long trousers. In summer, junior boys wear gray shorts and a sleeveless light blue shirt, with or without a gray pullover.[7] Senior boys are allowed long white trousers. Footwear is either black shoes with school stockings or black leather sandals, called *peshawaris*, with no stockings.[8] The turbans of Sikh boys must be either light or dark blue. The dominant "colors" so far (three of which, in fact, are non-colors) are blue, gray, black and white.

After classes there is a change into the games uniform. This uniform has already been described – deep blue shorts with a gray and blue shirt. It is followed by a change into evening clothing (white kurta-pajamas or white shirt and white trousers, with an optional gray pullover). Finally there is a change back into nightwear.

What is consistent throughout these many changes is the restriction to non-colors (gray–black–white) and blue. A certain logic may be observed in the amount of blue permitted. Blue, and especially the more saturated blue of the games uniform, is more closely associated with sports than with studies, where the non-colors prevail. The warmer colors only make an appearance in the red, yellow, green and blue singlets worn during some inter-house competitions. This suggests a more general link between color itself, the human body and physical activity. Color and skin color are thus offset against gray, the expression of mind and spirit. When the boys from all the different houses appear at athletics events, and at the annual PT competition, the effect is of a bursting out of color and animal energy.

We can construct a chart from some of the foregoing distinctions.

uniformity	individuality
institution	inhabitants
cloth	flesh
gray	blue
non-color	color
gray/blue	skin color
"cool" colors	"warm" colors
studies	sports
mind	body

Color is a major variable in the clothing worn at different times of day. It thus has an important role in the ordering of time, activities and age groups. If skin color represents the human body at its most natural, individual and vulnerable, then clothing is what covers it and contains it, expressing the forces of social and institutional control. Perhaps significantly, when the boys remove their uniforms for the evening bath they appear to remove many of the inhibitions and stresses of school along with them. At Doon this is a time of relaxation and sociability, no doubt enhanced, especially in winter, by the warm atmosphere of steam, soap and running water.[9] At the school what one wears indicates the activities one is permitted to do, just as what one does dictates what uniform one must wear. Clothing thus provides a set of signs about appropriate behavior and status. Secondary modifications of the uniforms restore a degree of individuality to the students by rewarding them with emblems of personal merit. A dark blue blazer is awarded for prowess in sport, a black blazer for high academic achievement, and house or school "colors" for related achievements, allowing one to wear various neckties, neck scarves and badges. The school delegates considerable power to Prefects and House Captains, who are allowed further variations of uniform and are given other privileges such as rooms to themselves.

Space, Time and Ritual

The attention I have given to color and uniforms would, I think, be disproportionate and unsustainable if these existed in isolation. However, the aesthetic principles of order and restraint that define the school's uniforms are consistent with a broader aesthetics to be found in other aspects of school life – its rituals, its living arrangements, its organization of time and the character of its buildings and grounds. The appeal to, and conditioning of, the senses can hardly account for the full shaping of the individual in all matters of taste, outlook and behavior, but by the same token it cannot be wholly separated from the rituals, manners and expectations that are part of a coherent and instrumental social system. And in some instances it is difficult to escape observing a close connection between, for example, an austere material existence, a subdued color scheme and a de-emphasizing of wealth and ostentation.

As with uniforms, the colors used inside school buildings are restricted. Floors are of cement or gray flagstones, walls are whitewashed, unrelieved by color except for the dark woodwork of the desks in the classrooms and colored bedcovers in the dormitories. In some rooms the bedcovers are green, in others blue, but the two are never mixed. The dormitories thus present an image of single colors offset against much larger areas of colorlessness. The use of green and blue maintains the contrast between cool and warm colors contained in A.E. Foot's distinction between the institution and the body. In the restricted, even grim, color scheme of the dormitories, skin color stands out as the chief sign of human vitality. But once asleep, the boys become encased in the green and blue bed linen of the institution.[10]

In parallel with the many changes of uniform required, the student's day is subdivided and highly regulated, leaving little time for unscheduled activities. This is not only meant to keep the boys out of trouble; there is a general sense that time not used in some

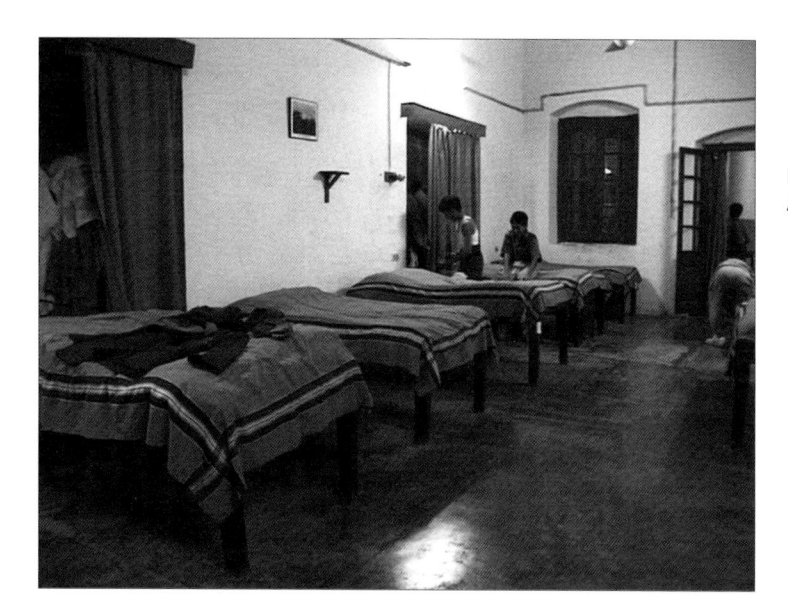

Figure 4
A Doon School Dormitory.

activity of self-improvement is time wasted. Indeed, the timetable is so crowded that students quite often find themselves required to attend two activities that meet at the same time. The regime was apparently more relaxed in the early days of the school, but even then the efficient use of time was pursued with characteristic thoroughness. In 1941 the headmaster observed

> While at school, [a boy] will sleep for nine hours in every twenty-four; he will work at his books for six hours; he will exercise his muscles for one and a half hours; he will eat for one and a half hours; he will wash for half an hour; he can allow half an hour for dressing and still there are five hours in each day.

Several other features of school life reflect a similar quasi-scientific attitude to numbers and measurement. It has been a long-standing practice to record the height and weight of each boy twice a year, although there no longer appears to be much practical application of this to health or diet. Each student is given a number upon joining the school. The numbers are used administratively for recording marks and keeping track of school clothing, but they are also used in daily life to call groups of students together. This is not to say that students' names are avoided, or that students feel depersonalized by their numbers, but that the numbering of students is accepted and perhaps even respected as a feature of modernity. Students take a certain pride in their numbers, which they sometimes incorporate into their email addresses and remember long after they have left the school.

Figure 5
Students at Assembly.

At assembly, students are grouped by age and size and stand in parallel rows along the edges of an open rectangular space, as shown in Figure 5. This symmetry and geometry of straight lines and right angles is carried over into the dormitories where beds are arranged in parallel or in squares of four. Such an arrangement is not unusual in boarding schools, but it represents an aesthetic choice. At some other Indian schools the students sit on the floor in concentric circles during assembly, and their beds are arranged unevenly around the walls of the dormitories.[11] At meals, Doon School students sit at tables arranged in parallel lines. They are grouped in the first instance by house and secondarily by age. The tables are white and the stainless steel plates and eating utensils produce a monotone of silver-gray not unlike the school uniforms.

Team sports such as football and hockey – rituals played out in rectangular spaces – occupy a great deal of time at the school, as does cricket with its calculus of wickets, runs and overs. Physical training at the school culminates in a competition at which houses vie for perfection in the formal arrangement of bodies (see Figure 6). Although the school's preference for square geometry appears to be based partly on an admiration for science it also has military precedents. A former headmaster of the school, John Mason, observed that

> The aesthetic of the school has been a very male ... somewhat physically-dominated aesthetic, or culture. I don't know if I'm being wildly sacrilegious in suggesting that this was an early twentieth century recipe for the ideal schoolboy. It may also

Figure 6
The Annual Physical Training Competition.

have something to do with the imperial view of leadership and ideal growth, and the mold that a society that looked at militancy as a way of expression expected its men to grow and behave.[12]

As this suggests, the expressive forms of an institution are not only a matter of cultural style or functionality but are closely linked to its history and ideological foundations. At Doon School, many of the aesthetic features that are observable on the surface of everyday life are mirrored in its most basic structures. Students joining the school enter a social system that differs in important respects from the Indian middle-class family life they have left behind. Distinctions of class, caste, religion and wealth are to a large extent suppressed, even if not altogether forgotten. Power is not so clearly exercised from above as it is in government; it is delegated to students in a system that sometimes resembles the British colonial strategy of "indirect rule." Each year the headmaster and teachers appoint new prefects and house captains. This produces a hierarchy determined partly by seniority, partly by perceived leadership qualities and partly by the practice of "scoping," in which Year 11 students seek to win approval (and rank) by making themselves conspicuously useful.

As they progress toward such rewards the students are divided into two main age groups. In the first three years (in D, B and C forms) one is a junior. During the last three years (A, S and Sc forms) one is a senior. As we have seen, this change is registered in one's clothing. Younger boys wear shorts for more activities, and their bodies are therefore generally more exposed than those of older boys. Older boys, perhaps in keeping with their social advancement, must appear in more fully institutional dress. The shift in status and uniform, which occurs approximately when one turns fifteen, underlines one of the school's most obvious but least acknowledged facts – that the single category of student has been stretched to include everything from small boys to near men.

The transformation of boys into men is part of the school's purpose, but it also poses a threat. Differences in uniforms for juniors and seniors recognize the changes taking place in the boys' bodies, but there is at the same time a certain resistance to this process on the part of the school authorities. One of the major problems facing boarding schools has resulted from the gradual prolongation of childhood. Its span has been extended with the advance of higher education and the delayed onset of work. Doon School's students range in age from eleven to eighteen. New boys entering the school are often described as "timid mice" by older students, but by the time they leave many are essentially adults, with the physical strength and sense of independence of grown men.[13] In what is already a hierarchical system the most senior boys often compete for power and influence with their teachers. To maintain its control, the school attempts to de-emphasize the process of maturation, or rather, to condense it, encouraging younger students to behave more like men and often restricting older students to the status and appearance of young boys. This is achieved partly by limiting the privileges of older students, partly by applying the school rules more or less universally to all and partly through clothing. For although older students sometimes wear the long trousers of adults, during games they must wear the same childish uniforms as the youngest boys. Conversely, the youngest boys are made to struggle into the woolen suits of the winter uniform, which are often too big for them.

As may now be apparent, Doon School's social structure involves three overlapping classificatory systems. Students are differentiated according to age, house affiliation and authority. To begin with, one is either a junior or a senior, depending upon which form one is in. Seniors can demand "favors" of juniors, a practice inherited from the fagging system of British public schools. Next comes one's house affiliation. There are five main houses, and although students in the first year live in special "holding houses" their future house affiliation has already been assigned. The third system distinguishes between those who, in their final year, hold positions of authority (as prefects and house captains) and those who do not. Prefects and house captains are given rooms to themselves, or "studies." They can order a punishment for almost anyone junior to them in the school. There is considerable competition for these positions and disgruntled students who are not appointed sometimes joke about belonging to NAPU, the mythical "Non-Appointed Prefects Union." Prefects and house captains in fact provide much of the day-to-day labor of administering the houses and supervising other activities in the school.

This system is essentially the one created by the founders of the school, although it is constantly being reindorsed and subtly modified by the students themselves – by older students, who have already been initiated into the system, and new students eager to fit in. Age, house affiliation and rank form a complex that is reflected visually and tactilely in many of the features of the school, such as its uniforms. These features form a sensory world that students are exposed to day after day. It is evident that the aesthetics of this system exerts an influence at several levels. If social structures dictate appearances, appearances also deepen and naturalize social structures, making the alternatives appear foreign and "unnatural." How one behaves, and what one approves, may thus be determined as much by aesthetic concerns – by the desire to preserve the living patterns and sensations one has become habituated to – as by functions that may by now have become outdated or even indefensible, such as "favors" and bullying. One's social and physical surroundings become increasingly expressive of their own existential properties and the associations that have been built up around them over time. In the process, a transferal of emotive power from the signified to the signifier takes place, sometimes even a reversal of meaning, as familiar stimuli take on a life of their own. Something disagreeable may become agreeable through its association with positive emotions of comradeship or belonging. In certain respects this is not unlike the hypothesis put forward by Darwin, and later by William James, that the expressive forms of the emotions, such as crying or smiling, may actually feed back into the subject and generate these emotions themselves. One ex-student told me that while he was at Doon some of his fellow students complained that the school was losing its boarding school identity and becoming more like a day school because bullying was on the decline!

The Character of a School
When it was founded in the 1930s Doon School reflected many of the underlying and contradictory complexities of British–Indian colonial relations. The school had been conceived as a British-style public school for upper middle-class Indian boys, in contrast to the existing boarding schools in India such as Bishop Cotton School in Simla, which catered primarily to British families, and the "Chiefs' Colleges," such as Mayo College in Rajasthan, which were for boys from Indian princely families. A number of the school's founders and supporters, including its guiding spirit Satish Ranjan Das, had attended public schools in England and their aim was to provide an equivalent form of education for the future leaders of an independent India. However, instead of studying Greek and Latin, the boys would study Hindi and Urdu. The school would be open to students of all castes, classes and religions. Doon students would be treated alike, living a simple, even Spartan life in communal dormitories, unlike students at the Chiefs' Colleges where some of the young princes

lived in mini-palaces surrounded by their servants. Vegetarians and non-vegetarians would eat together. Corporal punishment was banned – a progressive step at that time. An ethic of service to the nation and the local community was promoted. Education was to be based on scientific thought, free of ancient prejudices. The boys' minds and bodies would be trained to develop the qualities of endurance, leadership and fair play.

It is not entirely clear how Doon School came to adopt blue and gray as its colors, but as we have seen, that choice came to play a part in the school's conceptions of mind and body.[14] One theory, not confirmed, is that Mrs Foot, the wife of the first headmaster, chose the school colors, a choice possibly determined by what cloth was readily available. In the case of gray an obvious advantage was that it did not show the dirt. It is also possible that for the school's Indian founders, gray at some level stood for Britain – its weather, its churches and public buildings, and its elite educational institutions. Blue, on the other hand, was the color associated with the Hindu deities, especially Lord Krishna, and with the Brahman caste from which many of the founders came.[15] These men belonged to a professional class who admired what they saw as the British values of egalitarianism, self-discipline and scientific thought. They were, at the same time, anxious to assert their Indian (and, more specifically, Hindu) cultural heritage, and in fact many saw themselves as the restorers and custodians of a more enlightened Indian tradition, stripping away its layers of superstition and caste prejudice. This outlook characterized the "Bengal Renaissance," inspired by Raja Rammohan Roy and the Hindu reformist organization, the Brahmo Samaj, by artists and literary figures such as Tagore, and religious leaders such as Ramakrishna and Vivekananda. In one sense, then, blue and gray were not opposed but complementary. Each suggested distance from the unruly passions – blue as a color at the cooler end of the spectrum and gray as the repudiation of all color. Both would have been seen as appropriate to the future character of the school.

Although Doon School's specific combination of features may be unique and immediately recognizable to present students and old boys, it is hardly original. It has developed out of practices established in other schools and their institutional predecessors: seminaries, monasteries, military barracks, guilds and artisans' workshops. When it was created, Doon School was regarded as a novel experiment. Its founders had taken the British public school and refashioned it as an instrument of modern Indian identity. In many respects the school was meant to provide an answer to those who saw the colonial subject as backward-looking, passive and enfeebled. Doon School's emphasis on science and the disciplining of the body was part of the response and became part of its aesthetic orientation. Boys may have been dressed so as to organize and control them, but their uniforms were also meant to show them off. The blue games uniform, made of rough cotton cloth, provided a contrasting frame for shining, healthy bodies. Identical uniforms emphasized the orderliness of the boys when they were massed in formation for assemblies, meals, physical training or "callover" (rollcall). Such images were the visual correlatives of the school's ideal of a rational existence.

The school's strategy for teaching manners, character and citizenship became evident in the first few years. The intention was to create the conditions in which certain values would flourish and be gradually absorbed by the boys. The study of science was believed to have pervasive effects on character. As the Chief Guest at the Founder's Day celebrations of 1948 put it, "it is wrong to think that science teaches only science. Science brings about a change in the whole attitude of boys. It brings about correct judgment, alertness and obedience to laws."[16] Environment, example and peer pressure were considered more effective than discipline, and indeed A.E. Foot wrote that "we believe that character-training is more a matter of organisation than instruction... The purpose is achieved not by precept or instruction, but by creating an environment in which a boy is led to do things for himself."[17] Nevertheless, Foot was not above issuing advice and homilies to reinforce the principle of environmental learning. Boys were expected to monitor their own progress and make the necessary corrections. The school's program thus implied a double imperative: first, to mold the individual through exposure to a carefully constructed social aesthetic and, second, to encourage among students the conscious perfection of the self.

Although Doon School, when it opened, may have appeared to be the culmination of an evolutionary process, it soon became a step in a new one. As time went on, more and more Indian schools were patterned on Doon or gradually adopted its practices. This came about partly by example and partly through the dispersal of Doon teachers to other schools as masters and headmasters. It also reflected the underlying ties of power and ideology. The values that the school espoused in its early years became institutionalized in the politics of the postcolonial period, especially in the Congress party. The connections are not hard to find. A Doon School boy, Rajiv Gandhi, was later to become Prime Minister. The Doon School song, Tagore's *Jana Gana Mana*, was to become India's national anthem.

Aesthetics in Society

It is difficult to know precisely how exposure to a particular color or set of colors over six years might influence a student, either at the time or later in life. It is reasonable to assume that exposure to any sensory environment, apart from making it increasingly familiar, is closely tied to other experiences, either pleasant or unpleasant. If you were unhappy at Doon, blue-and-gray might evoke all the things you feared and hated; it might trigger a nasty reaction in the pit of your stomach. If you enjoyed yourself, it might lift your spirits and recall moments of comradeship and triumph. One student told me that his father, a Doon graduate, had a decided preference for blue shirts. A more recent graduate said that he felt an aversion to blue but was attracted to gray, a clue, perhaps, that he was drawn more to the ethos of studies than to sports. But the quality of such responses is not necessarily the most important thing about them. Even if one suffers, emblems of past suffering may become valuable as points of reference, preserving links between one's history and the person one has become.

I have written selectively about certain features of Doon School life, color being among the most abstract of these. However, focusing on a single feature always runs the risk of placing it in an unrealistically prominent light. When experiencing sensations such as color, one does not ordinarily isolate them from the broader tapestry of objects and activities in which they are enmeshed. The surroundings of a chosen detail or quality tend to reassert themselves. How, then, can one single out some quality for attention without depriving it of the connections and, precisely, the unremarked qualities that it possesses in daily life? Unless one isolates the detail, one cannot see it properly; but one cannot see it properly if one isolates it. An exclusive focus on one aspect of life begins to erode its normality, its connectedness.

And yet it is through the study of such discrete aspects of life in their varied contexts that we are likely to learn the most about the socially-generated systems that structure our sensory experience and ultimately influence our attitudes and actions. Examining the role of color in a number of communities is one way in which we might begin to search for a more general theory of social aesthetics. Although we acknowledge major differences in the ways in which societies deal with sensory experience, we tend to regard these as the concomitant effects of material conditions and patterns of cultural diffusion. And, although it is true that these factors may underlie the variations in aesthetic systems, they do not explain why these systems exist in the first place, nor indeed how they evolve, how they influence political and economic decisions and how they bear upon the personal lives of individuals.

In acknowledging that aesthetics plays a role in society, we must also accept that it may have more profound effects, both culturally and historically. Certain combinations of sensory stimuli appear to play a significant part in reinforcing patriotic and other mass sentiments. One need only recall here the use of color and ritual in 1930s Germany which, although replete with ascribed symbolic meanings (for example, red and black representing blood and soil), clearly exerted a more generalized power. A fuller understanding of the social role of aesthetics may thus benefit studies of nationalism, ethnicity, warfare, religion and sectarian politics. Current studies in body praxis and "rhetoric culture" may eventually be seen as closely allied to the study of social aesthetics.

A number of questions deserve our attention. Can sensory environments be categorized in any systematic way, and if so by what criteria? To what extent do these environments operate as systems – that is to say, do they have an ecology? In studying them, should we look first for their dominant effects, for their structures or for the senses to which they appeal? What are the forms of response to specific aesthetic patterns? What are the prolonged effects of these patterns on individuals and populations and how do they change over time? What are the processes by which they are modified through internal agency or external pressures? Do particular combinations of features emerge through chance, or natural selection, or conscious choice? When we begin to address such questions we may be closer to realizing what Baumgarten envisaged as a "science of sensory cognition."

Acknowledgments
My thanks to David Howes, Judith MacDougall, Howard Morphy, Lucien Taylor, Diana Young and Nicolas Peterson for reading earlier drafts of this article and providing helpful comments.

Notes
1. Dai Vaughan notes that this image may also imply concealment and competition. "We may reflect that the back of a playing card is the side held towards others until the decisive moment of win-or-lose" (Vaughan 2005: 458).
2. A distinction is often made between chromatic and achromatic colors, the latter consisting of black, white and gray. Chromatic colors are considered to have three components: hue (referring to their wavelength in the light spectrum); value (their lightness or darkness, or luminance); and chroma (the intensity of their hue). Within this system, a color without hue will appear gray and thus may not be considered a color in the fullest sense. All languages possess a name for at least one of the achromatic colors, along with varying numbers of names for the chromatic colors. For a detailed study of these cultural variations see Berlin and Kay's influential *Basic Color Terms* (1969).
3. For the purposes of this article, a color without hue will be characterized as a non-color.
4. John Gage, citing the color of gas flames in heaters, observes that, contrary to the popular belief that the color red signals heat, "the short-wave, high-frequency energy of the blue-violet end of the spectrum signals the greatest capacity to heat, and the long-wave, low-frequency red end, the least" (1999: 22). However, cultural associations of color with temperature are not entirely unconnected, for the wavelengths of red and yellow do lie closer to the infra-red end of the spectrum, the wavelength of heat. And although associations of temperature with color vary considerably across cultures there is a general consensus among them

that supports a subjective or physiological connection. Values for the wavelengths of the "standard" colors vary from one source to another, but a typical chart shows them (in nanometers) as follows:

Color	Wavelength
Red	780–622 nm
Orange	622–597 nm
Yellow	597–577 nm
Green	577–492 nm
Blue	492–455 nm
Violet	455–390 nm

5. The school's first two residential dormitories to be built, Kashmir House and Hyderabad House, are of whitish stone with red arches, red detailing and red roofs. When Foot House and Martyn House, the school's original "holding houses" for first year students, were recently demolished and rebuilt, the new buildings were of red brick with red roofs.
6. Clothing is used in the school as a means of punishment. The most common punishment is the "change-in-break." It is given for minor infractions, such as making one's bed badly or having unpolished shoes. If caught, the boy is given a chit and must run back to his house during the mid-morning break and change into his PT (physical training) uniform. He must then run back to the main building to have the chit signed, return to the house, change into his school clothes again and return to have the chit signed a second time. If he lives in a nearby house he may have to change into his games clothes as well and run two more times with two more signings.
7. Doon School shorts are quite long, in the British colonial fashion, reaching to just above the knee.
8. Peshawaris have recently been replaced by high-tech sandals.
9. Communal bathing with other boys has been the norm at the school from the beginning, perhaps to underline the school's values of openness and equality. Although it runs counter to prevailing Indian notions of modesty, and indeed may be an importation from British public schools, most boys seem to accept and enjoy it after overcoming their initial shyness. However, one boy reported to me his feeling of shock at seeing a sexually mature boy naked for the first time. When, at a recent School Council meeting, one student suggested converting the open showers into cubicles, the minutes read "The Chairman felt that it was a tradition that had never been questioned. Moreover, open showering enhanced hygiene and maturity. The cost of maintaining cubicles would be enormous and they wouldn't be hygienic either. It was decided to remain with the present system." (School Council Minutes, April 14, 2006.)

10. One of Berlin and Kay's observations was that the number of color terms used in small or medium-scale societies was more limited than in larger and more technically complex ones. Is it possible that Doon School, as a small-scale (and, in Turner's terms, non-exchange) society observes a similar limitation, but in its color usage rather than its terminology?
11. I observed more circular arrangements at both The Centre for Learning near Bangalore and at Rishi Valley School, a Krishnamurti Foundation school in Andhra Pradesh.
12. Quoted from the film *Doon School Chronicles* (2000), scenes 58–60.
13. As might be expected, the usual sorts of early adolescent sexual activity occur between boys at the school, but, as in other boarding schools, there have also been cases of sexual abuse practiced by older boys on younger ones.
14. A.E. Foot favored cotton cloth of Indian manufacture, for toughness, hygiene and the support of local industries. The choice of colors would also have been influenced by the need to avoid colors already in use by nearby schools.
15. Sanjay Srivastava (1998: 116) maintains that a Hindu aesthetic persists strongly at Doon School in its rituals and emblems, despite its professed secularism. He argues that such emblems retain an indelible aura of their history. While he only discusses the religious connotations of white in school rituals, a similar argument could be made for the uses of blue. He observes: "It is crucial, then, to understand that the process of the ensconcement of the School's official ideology of secularism within the contours of a Hindu system of meanings … was initiated in its earliest days" (123).
16. The Governor General of the United Provinces, Shri Rajagopalachari, quoted in *The Doon School Weekly*, October 30, 1948.
17. *The Doon School Book*, 1949, reprinted in Chopra 1996: 40.

References

Berlin, Brent and Kay, Paul. 1969. *Basic Color Terms*. Berkeley: University of California Press. Reprinted 1991 with an updated bibliography by Luisa Maffi.

Chopra, Pushpindar Singh (ed.). 1996. *The Doon School Sixty Years On*. Dehra Dun: The Doon School Old Boys Society.

Gage, John. 1999. *Colour and Meaning: Art, Science and Symbolism*. London: Thames and Hudson.

MacDougall, David. 2000. *Doon School Chronicles* [film]. Centre for Cross-Cultural Research, Australian National University. 140 minutes.

Srivastava, Sanjay. 1998. *Constructing Post-Colonial India: National Character and the Doon School*. London and New York: Routledge.

Turner, Terence. 1995. "Social Body and Embodied Subject: Bodiliness, Sociality, and Subjectivity among the Kayapo." *Cultural Anthropology*, 10(2): 143–70.
Vaughan, Dai. 2005. "The Doon School Project." *Visual Anthropology*, 18: 457–64.

Seeing Isn't Believing: Blindness, Race, and Cultural Literacy

Elaine Gerber

Dr Gerber is an assistant professor of Anthropology at Montclair State University in New Jersey. She formerly served as the Senior Research Associate at the American Foundation for the Blind. gerbere@mail.montclair.edu

ABSTRACT   This article focuses on audio description (a technique used for "translating" visual material to aural readers/blind people) and its relation to the cultural construction of race in the United States. In it, I present exploratory research on audio description (AD) and raise important questions in the field of visual anthropology: how does one translate visual material for a non-seeing audience? From the point of view of blind consumers, what constitutes "good" description? What is culturally salient in the visual field? Is race important to describe? This paper presents the results of three telephone focus groups on AD, conducted in the USA in the fall of 2005. The focus groups involved thirty-nine blind or visually impaired people nationwide, who discussed (among other things) the need for race to be described. These participants argued for the need for race-based knowledge as an important part of cultural literacy, and, in so doing, raised questions about how visual race is.

KEYWORDS: audio description, visual culture, race, blindness

Introduction

Consider ... two boys rapidly contracting the eyelids of their right eyes. In one, this is an involuntary twitch; in the other, a conspiratorial signal to a friend. The two movements are, as movements, identical; from an I-am-a-camera, "phenomenalistic" observation of them alone, one could not tell which was a twitch and which was a wink, or indeed whether both or either was a twitch or a wink. Yet the difference, however unphotographical, between a twitch and a wink is vast...

(Geertz, *The Interpretation of Cultures*)

This article is about Audio Description (a technique used for "translating" visual material to aural "readers," most of whom are primarily blind people) and its relationship to the cultural construction of race in the United States.[1] In general, we live in an incredibly visual world and most of the time, therefore, this presumes a cultural readership which can see (one only need to recall the utterly visual nature of the news coverage following Hurricane Katrina in the USA, where pictures alone were left to describe the color of poverty in America). Instead, this article flips that on its head and asks us to consider what the implications of visual content are for a non-visual audience. In so doing, it addresses some of the larger questions about difference, speaking simultaneously to the social nature of disability (Oliver 1990; Davis 1997; Linton 1998; Barnes, Mercer and Shakespeare 1999) and the cultural construction of race.

Background on Audio Description

More specifically, audio description (AD), also called video description and DVS®,[2] is the verbal narration of non-verbal content (for example, settings, gestures) inserted between dialogue in various media. By providing "radio-quality pictures" it is often described as being to the blind what closed captioning is to the Deaf. Just as closed captioning – which began as a unique technology for the Deaf – can now be found in gyms and congressional offices as well as whenever anyone tries to "mute" the commercials on their standard television set, AD also has "universal design" appeal, such as allowing sighted viewers to follow their favorite program without seeing the screen (for instance when driving or in another room preparing dinner). Already its reach is quite broad: in the United States alone there are over 225 mainstream cinemas offering AD (National Center for Accessible Media 2006) and Amazon.com offers nearly 150 videos with audio description (although the number of DVDs available is far smaller). In 2002, the Federal Communications Commission required the major networks and cable channels to present at least four hours of described programming per week. Although this was struck down in court, there is a residual amount of AD on television, mostly on a voluntary basis, and two bills currently before Congress seek to restore the FCC's rules. At present there are hundreds of programs (and many more movies) televised each week with AD via the Secondary Audio Programming (SAP) feature (SAP is an auxiliary audio channel for television that can be broadcast or transmitted both over the air and by cable TV; it is often used for an alternate, or second language as well as for audio description), and AD is offered for many live theater and dance performances, as well as accompanying museum exhibits.

Despite its widespread presence, the "field" of Audio Description is in its infancy. There is only a handful of small companies in the United States who produce AD, and there is no formal training program for those wanting to become describers.[3] At the same time, it is anticipated that as this technology becomes more mainstream and as the nation's population ages, the prevalence and uses of AD will grow tremendously. Moreover, evidence exists that the benefits of AD extend beyond blind people to people with learning disabilities, people learning English as a second language and many others, including sighted viewers in such situations as are described above (Bridge Multimedia 2006). The need for additional research on (and training in) AD is at a critical juncture.

There is a limited set of "best practices" developed by professionals in the industry as to how to do description (see ADI 2006, Clark 2001).[4] However, these – at least as developed in the United States – have been designed without much formal input by blind consumers, nor with much theoretical sophistication. Both are problematic. One clear guideline states that description should never interfere with existing dialogue. Therefore, there is limited space in which to do the description. In other words, not everything will be able to be described in the time permitted. And this raises questions as to what it is most salient to describe. Second, the "gold standard" most used in training new describers is, literally, to "say what you see" (ADI 2006). Now, from a theoretical standpoint, this is highly problematic: put ten sighted people in a room and ask them to describe something, and you are going to get at least ten different descriptions. Clearly, what is "seen" is different for everyone and depends on who is doing the seeing and in what contexts (Berger 2005; Hockey 2006).

Moreover, these "best practices" regarding AD, at present, do not explicitely address culture, race or ethnic context, except to say that one should describe "the physical appearance of the character" and "not use offensive or racist terms, but ... describe ethnicity where relevant" (ADI 2006). Further, there is a stated belief among this community that description should not be interpretive (in part this arises from the need to appease copyright laws and Hollywood producers that providing an AD track was not altering the original "art" in any way, that it is not a *new* cultural medium/artistic production). While perhaps practical, this has created an ongoing theoretical tension about how best to do description, in circumstances in which there is ambiguity. (It may also limit the potential for this technique in creating new artistic genres, but that is a separate discussion). Geertz' example above (the difference between a twitch versus a wink versus "rapidly contracting his right eyelids" versus "practicing a burlesque of a friend faking a wink to deceive an innocent into thinking a conspiracy is in motion" [1973:7]) accurately reaches to the heart of the problem in description. The audio describer is in a sense an ethnographer making meaning out of what is there. Yet, blind people – as articulated in this research and elsewhere (see ADI listserv archives) – do not want interpretation, but need "thick description" (Geertz 1973).

Questions about ambiguity are particularly problematic in the case of facial expressions, but they apply to the issues of "race" as well. How does one describe "racial ambiguity," for instance people who visibly do not fit into a single specifiable "race" or who intentionally play with this ambiguity in order to "pass"? Because there are groups who run the phenotypic spectrum (for example, Cubans, Dominicans, Puerto Ricans and others), the use of AD can contribute to broader sociological and anthropological understandings of the "other." At the same time, theories of race highlight the difference between describing phenotype and describing "race." Although questions about race surface from time to time informally on blindness listservs, the "field" of AD, such as it is, remains under-researched and theoretically unsophisticated, not only about race but also about "seeing." Yet there is some very informative anthropological and historical scholarship that has explored the relationship between race and the senses, including vision, on which to draw (see e.g., Classen 1998; Howes 2003, 2005; Berger 2005; Smith 2006a).

Consequently, this research sought to expand on what limited existing research there is on AD (Packer and Kirchner 1997; Piety 2004), and particularly to explore what constitutes "good description" from the point of view of blind consumers. (Further applied results from the research that address existing guidelines appear elsewhere.) Thus, this research raises a number of key questions including "How much description is too much?" and "What happens to the medium if description is built in from the beginning, can it shape the kind of art that is produced?" However, because I am an anthropologist, I am particularly interested in what is culturally salient in the visual field and focus this paper accordingly on whether race is important to describe. In so doing, this work speaks to questions about the nature of embodied difference and the presumption of the normative body (that is to say, a sighted audience). Blind people as "aural readers" of cultural texts have much to teach about the cultural construction of race.

Methodology

This paper presents the results of three telephone focus groups on audio description that were conducted in September/October 2005, involving a total of thirty-nine blind or visually impaired adults from across the United States. (This research involved both blind and visually impaired consumers; since my point is not to make a distinction between levels of vision, however, for purposes of shorthand I refer to both sets of people throughout the paper as "blind.") Each group lasted from one-and-a-half to two hours, were audio-taped and then the recordings were transcribed. Participants were selected on a first-come, first-serve basis from over 250 responses to one email sent to a single listserv. (Clearly, this was an issue that resonated among this constituency.) Individuals were screened, gave their consent and were then assigned into one of three distinct focus groups: (a) individuals who had never seen (in order to ascertain whether their description needs were different from those individuals who could still see or who had a visual memory), (b) individuals who had a preference for or experience with description of live theater/dance (this was regardless of vision status as live description has exigencies unique to that format) and (c) those with a preference for or experience with description of TV/video/DVD/film, again regardless of vision status (although none of this research included sighted users). Although primarily white, the sample of participants varied by race, age, gender, ethnicity, employment status, household income and State of residence. Each person received an honorarium for their participation.

The Cultural Construction Of Race

Anthropologists believe that race is a cultural construction. Simply put, there is no biological basis for race. Cultural categories of race vary from place to place: people sort one another into racial categories according their local culture's instructions. For example, in France, the term, "*les Blacks*" refers to people from the African continent, including North Africa (people whom Americans would refer to as Arab, not Black). My graduate school advisor, a fair-skinned African American woman spent several years as a "white woman," according to the cultural conceptions of the local people in Zaire with whom she was working. Another colleague calls herself "Indian" because she is from India, but is often labeled as "Asian" when she travels to Britain. And these are not simply differences in word choice. Research has shown that in Brazil (see Harris 1970; Kottak and Kozaitis 2003), for example, the terms for race are more flexible than they are in the United States, that Brazilians use many more of them than do Americans and that they do not rely on the rule of hypodescent. (In Brazil, children from the same parents can be classified as belonging to different races if they appear phenotypically different, whereas, in the United States, even "one drop" of mixed blood assigns someone to minority status.) Further, in Brazil, race is something that can change over the course of a person's lifetime, especially if there is a change in class status (hence the Brazilian expression that "money whitens"), whereas race in the United States is something one is "born with" and is unchanging.

That is not to say that race is not a significant category. It is. It is just that it is a cultural, not biological phenomenon. This is analogous to the argument proposed by scholars of disability (Groce 2005; Kleege 1999; Linton 1998): while impairment may be biological, the sorting, or determining to which group of disabled people a person belongs, varies from place to place (for example, twins are not considered "disabled" in the United States but they are to the Ashanti; likewise, people labeled as "partially sighted" in mainstream America might not be considered disabled among the Amish). In other words, "racializing" people is learned (Mullings 2005: 674). And, in the United States blind people learn how to racialize people just as sighted people do. Moreover, racial categories used in the United States are significant for blind people, whether or not they can see those differences for themselves.

Findings

"It does kind of have something to do with it because a sighted person can look at the TV and say 'oh, she looks foreign or oh, he looks African American' and we don't know that."

"I don't want to have to spend a lot of mental time figuring out something that the sighted person can see in a glance. For example, I don't want in the middle of the play to go 'oh he's African American and that's important.'"

Overwhelmingly, the blind people participating in this study wanted to know races of characters in film, on TV, in the movies and cast in theater. These participants argued for the need for race-based knowledge as an important part of cultural literacy. As many of them said, they wanted to know race if it was salient. So the question becomes: what is salient? When is race salient?

Race as Central to the Plot
Unanimously, emphatically and without question, participants wanted to know about the race of characters portrayed on the screen and

stage. This was particularly true if they felt it was central to the plot. Marcus (a pseudonym, as are the rest of the participants' names) explained:

> I think its very important if race has anything to do with it ... that you should say a Hispanic or a Latin person or an Asian person... Like in *My Greek Wedding*, he's the only non-Greek person in the living room full of these Greek people.[5]

Suzie concurred:

> You don't always know and it may not be important, but lets say it's a movie like, *A Patch of Blue*, it's very important to know that Sidney Poitier is black. You can't always tell; his dialogue is very well spoken. It's very hard to discern if he's black, but because of that particular movie, you've got to know.

Vickie gave another concrete example:

> There have been other experiences where I had a completely different feeling when I thought somebody was African American, and when I heard the description, I found out they weren't, and that changed what I thought was going on in the movie... In *Field of Dreams*, I had seen it without description and had drawn my own conclusions about the power and the meaning of the movie. Then I watched it with the description and I found out that Kirk Douglas played the doctor, which I didn't know, and I thought that that character was African American. So to talk about an African American doctor going through what he did, living in a small town in the south, was really powerful and precious for me. When they said it was Kirk Douglas, who I knew was Caucasian, it changed the whole entire premise of the movie for me.

So, if race is salient, is it necessary to describe? Can blind viewers already discern it, if it is not described? Some linguistics research (Massey and Lundy 2001) emerging out of the "ebonics controversy" in Oakland, California in the 1990s found that Americans can discern – and therefore discriminate – based solely on speech (for example, realtors have declined to take on certain clients, or banks to make mortgage offers *over the phone*). This supports the point made by Kudlick (2006) that "in some cases non-visual cues (particularly voice and context) helped blind people determine someone's race." However, the truth was, at least for these blind participants, that they could not always determine race by speech, as illustrated in the cases above. While there was clearly overwhelming agreement that these participants wanted to know race, there was discrepancy about whether race could be discerned accurately without description.

Kevin, who may have been more sensitive to vocal "otherness" since he lived in Maine (where the population is, as he described it, "mostly white") said that race wasn't important to describe "because you can tell what race they are normally when they open their mouth." Regional associations (South, Midwest, Northeast and West) – for largely historical reasons – are quite important in the United States. For example, the experience of slavery rendered Southern whites extremely sensitive to "sight and race" (Smith 2006a), and it is likely that these legacies would be different in northern regions, including those that were perceived as "mostly white" communities (see also Frankenberg 1993).

Others in the group, however, disagreed that race could be inferred from speech. Miguel, for example, did so wholeheartedly: "I know white people that sound totally black and black people who sound white." Others on the phone concurred, citing him as an example: that they would have assumed he was Latino by his name, but judging by his voice, they couldn't tell. Moreover, these issues become increasingly complex when brought into an international or cross-cultural context. For example, if an American blind person were watching a film with a black British actor in it, they would hear "nationality," or possibly "class" but not race; they hear a "British" accent, not someone who is "black." (In fact, I would wager that, because of traditional associations between British English, Old World money and a general perception of the stratification and workings of British society, that most non-sighted listeners would assume the actor was white, regardless of the type of British accent spoken.)

Race as Politically Central
When I asked if they wanted to know about race, even if it's not pertinent to the plot, the majority of these participants still wanted to know. They argued that race is always salient, regardless of whether it is central to the plot, because it is central to our culture.

Mary contested this point. She claimed, since there is only so much time in which to do the description, that:

> Frankly, I don't need to know that "the black waiter puts the plate down." I don't need to know every single person and what their race is. If it's not pertinent to the story then I don't need to know that.

Others disagreed, suggesting that it was always pertinent – in this cultural and historical moment – to know whether, following on her example, all low socio-economic positions are held by people of color. Eve exclaimed, "This isn't *Gone With the Wind*! When is it not significant that "all waiters are black?!" Vicky added:

> Well I think that not describing people that are Caucasian is assuming that we assume everybody is Caucasian unless you tell us that they're not. And I think it's more holistic and more respectful of all cultural diversity to actually go with [describing] everybody. Because that's not the way it's done now. The description assumes the person is white unless they tell us that they're not.

Eve continued:

> All the characters need to be described not just the African Americans or the Asians, but the Caucasians too, in terms of knowing and also not creating some kind of bias. I think it would be more … if we're concerned about appearing racist, I think it would be more racist to leave those things out because it shows a sort of hypersensitivity, or an aversion to race.

Miguel stated that there is also part of the politics that is identity based: "As a Hispanic person, I'm always interested in how many Hispanic actors are gonna get parts, what roles." Sasha elaborated on this point:

> If it was a really big part for an African American actor – say they had to fight really hard to win – maybe that's part of the acknowledgement they'd like. If you just leave it out, it is kind of doing us a disservice…. It's no different from wanting to know if someone has a disability or other obstacle.

There are very few roles for disabled people to play and even fewer successful disabled actors in Hollywood. The knowledge that these roles are being played by someone with a disability – or other minority roles played by a person of color – is actually very important cultural information. These describe our cultural moment – not just in period pieces or foreign geographies. According to theater studies, during an earlier period of theater history, roles were based on the strength of performance (that is, men played female roles, women played male roles). More recently, theater and film in the United States entered an era of realism (in which actors have to look the part they are going to play – for instance, if you're black you have to play a black character). Therefore, it is an inherently political act and there is value in knowing, if there has been either "color-blind casting" or what is called "non-traditional casting" (in which, for example, a disabled person is playing a non-disabled role, since it is far more common that a non-disabled actor plays the scant few, disabled parts). So it is important to know if, as a society, we are moving beyond the "realism" phase, in which people are able to play roles that are not necessarily defined by their physical traits. Jesse was articulate about this point:

The fact of the disability or race or whatever is significant because it says something about our cultural blending, it says something about the sensitivity of the director. I want to know that. It's important culturally how roles are cast. It says something about the changing of our cultural norms. If there is a person, for example, who uses wheelchair for mobility, where that doesn't play a part in the character. It's significant that that person is in a wheelchair because, wow, another barrier is down. If they are playing a white man and a black woman as a couple, where the race does not enter into the play, it nonetheless says something about the theater, the director, and the culture.

In sum, because of the analogy to disability, many in these groups understood the value of having all races described, because even when it was not essential to a proper understanding of the plot, it demonstrated a wider social significance (and they discussed technical ways to convey that information, even if there was insufficient space in between the standard dialogue, such as creating "e-descriptions" online).

Race as Cultural Literacy

Lastly, the reason race is salient has to do with issues of cultural literacy. For example, even if a blind person does not know what a "smirk" looks like first-hand (although the majority of blind people in the United States have seen at some point in their lives and many have visual memories), one still knows or can know what a "smirk" means, what the significance of it is. There are many things that have cultural saliency of which blind people should be informed, even if they have not necessarily seen it for themselves. Directors may choose to bathe a scene in a blue glow or place a red light above a doorway for a reason; blind people understand the color symbolism even if they cannot perceive the red or blue themselves. They have a right to know what everyone else in the culture is picking up on, even if it does not mean anything, visually, to them. Derisha exclaimed, "That's exactly what I am saying! Whether the race has anything to do with the play or not, it is important, because it's what everyone else sees."

I argue this is an issue of cultural literacy. People must be fluent in their cultural tongue even if they cannot see an item for themselves: to deny people access to certain information further disables them. As Maya said, "I want to know because the sighted people know. Why shouldn't I know? And, If you're gonna talk to sighted people about the film..." This is particularly true regarding race. This issue of cultural literacy is important, because – like it or not – race is an important organizing factor in our society. Jane elaborated:

I agree, because Tiger Woods, for some reason I thought he was white. Then I found out he was black and I was like OOPPPS. And just to be in synch with everyone else. I mean ... any of the primary characteristics that you see, boom, in a flash, I want to know that. I am not going to know if he's black, or Hispanic, or Asian, or extraordinarily tall or extraordinarily thin. The primary characteristics of what you see visually, that's important ... it's important culturally in our society. Whether it should be or not, it is.

Granted there is evidence to challenge the underlying assumption that sighted people "know" race when they see it. In addition to the sources cited above and other literature on "passing," there is ample public discussion (for example, about the ability to identify potential terrorists based on their appearance [Smith 2006b]) and a variety of cultural forms taking these issues head on (e.g., consider the reality TV show, "Black.White," as shown on FX [see www.fxnetworks.com]), all of which challenge the notion that race can be "seen" by sighted people. In other words, those sighted people doing the description might be wrong. Or, at the very least, they need to be alert to the potential (and sometimes intentional) ambiguity of racializing people based on phenotype, that sometimes "seeing shouldn't be believing." The fact is, one can't always tell what one sees. Descriptions could take this assumption into account, for example, by stating "in walks a person of color..." or "in walks, what appears to be, a person of color..." as opposed to "in walks a black man."

Nonetheless, not providing this [racial] information, perpetuates the oppression of blind people, specifically through the association of blindness with a lack of knowledge – for not knowing the "obvious" – when, in fact, it is really a lack of access to information. (Barriers to information access are often conflated with the impairment itself, seeming to arise from a function of one's bodily condition rather than from structural and social conditions.) Simply, without cultural literacy, there can be no cultural equality. Or, as Charles Crawford, former President of the American Council of the Blind, put it, "to be the mainstream you've got to have access to TV" (2002).

Discussion and Conclusion

Creating a Color-Blind World

Are blind people less racist? Can they be? Isn't it just perpetuating racism to describe race? One could argue, counter to what these blind participants claimed, that, rather than "needing to know race," the opportunity exists, through description, to create a color-blind society. That blind people are (or will be) inherently less racist, as a result of less access to visual, skin-color based discrimination.

Research into America as a "color-blind society" found that more white students believed we are already living in a "post-race" era than students of color, who continued to feel that race remains current and central to their lives (Gallagher 2006: 96–100). Accordingly, one might assume that blind people of color would desire to know the race of actors on screen and stage, and blind white people might favor post-race, color-blind descriptions, yet this was not born out by my research participants, the majority of whom were white. Future research could examine this further, as well as explore what additional culturally salient circumstances exist, since these are likely to vary according to race, class, urban/suburban divisions and other features.

Nonetheless, what does appear important is that the "politics of casting" and the "politics of color" appear to be very important to the majority of blind people in this study, because (a) there are times when it is central to the storyline or setting, (b) it is deemed to be generally politically relevant and (c) that it serves as a foundation for cultural fluency about race (they need to understand the world the same way as sighted people, even if it is a racist world). It is an issue of equality.

In closing, I offer this description of the importance that accurate audio description affords Barbara:

> It is an educational tool, as well, because when we go to work or wherever we are with sighted people, we can talk about things that we would otherwise perhaps not know... It is very important because it allows us to have social integration that we might not otherwise have. ... It enables me to laugh when everyone else is laughing because I actually know what's going on. I guess it gives me a sense of, I don't know, power, cause I get to laugh too.

In sum, this paper raises questions about how visual race is and whether blind people can be liberated from the tyranny of an oppressive cultural discourse on race to become – so to speak – colorblind, or whether, as cultural subjects demanding equal exposure to all discourse, blind people are further perpetuating a racist system.

Notes
1. The author would like to thank the New School University's Faculty Development Fund, the American Foundation for the Blind, and Montclair State University for their support of this research.
2. DVS, or Descriptive Video Service, is a trademark name for the services produced by the Media Access Group at WGBH in Boston, MA.
3. A one-time seminar was hosted by Penn State University. Most training, when it exists, is conducted for new employees, or on a contractual basis by companies producing AD.

4. The United Kingdom has its own set of guidelines (see: www.ofcom.org.uk/static/archive/itc/itc_publications/codes_guidance/audio_description/index.asp.html)
5. This point reflects the frequent blurring of the terms, race and ethnicity, common throughout the United States.

References

Audio Description International (ADI). *Guidelines for Audio Description*. Accessed May 30, 2006 from http://www.adinternational.org/ADIguidelines.html.

Barnes, C., Mercer, G. and Shakespeare, T. 1999 *Exploring Disability: A Sociological Introduction*. Cambridge: Polity.

Berger, M.A. 2005. *Sight Unseen: Whiteness and American Visual Culture*. Berkeley: University of California Press.

Bridge Multimedia. *Universally Accessible Media: Audio Description*. Accessed July 19, 2006, from http://bridgemultimedia.com/audiodesc.php.

Clark, J. 2001. *Media Access: Standard Techniques in Audio Description*. November 26, 2001. Accessed May 30, 2006, from http://joeclark.org/access/description/ad-principles.html.

Classen, C. 1998. *The Color of Angels*. New York: Routledge.

Crawford, C. 2002. As quoted in Ellen Klugman, "Vision Quest: The Battle over Audio Description for the Blind." *TV Guide* (December 28).

Davis, L. 1997. *The Disability Studies Reader*. New York: Routledge.

Frankenberg, R. 1993. *The Social Construction Of Whiteness: White Women, Race Matters*. Minneapolis: University Of Minnesota Press.

Gallagher, C.A. 2006. "Color-Blind Privilege: The Social and Political Functions of Erasing the Color Line in Post Race America." In E. Higginbotham and M.L. Anderson (eds), *Race and Ethnicity in Society: The Changing Landscape.* Stamford: Thompson Wadsworth.

Geertz, C. 1973. *The Interpretation of Cultures*. New York: Basic Books Inc.

Groce, N.E. 2005. *Everyone Here Spoke Sign Language: Hereditary Deafness on Martha's Vineyard*. Cambridge MA: Harvard University Press.

Harris, M. 1970. "Referential Ambiguity in the Calculus of Brazilian Racial Identity." *Southwestern Journal of Anthropology,* 26(1): 1–14.

Hockey, J. 2006. "Sensing the Run: The Senses and Distance Running." *The Senses and Society*, 1(2): 183–201.

Howes, D. 2003. *Sensual Relations: Engaging the Senses in Culture and Social Theory*. Ann Arbor: University of Michigan Press.

———. 2005. *Empire of the Senses: The Sensual Culture Reader*. Oxford: Berg.

Kleege, G. 1999. *Sight Unseen*. New Haven: Yale University Press.

Kottak, C.P. and Kozaitis, K.A. 2003. *On Being Different: Diversity and Multiculturalism in the North American Mainstream* (2nd edn). New York: McGraw Hill.

Kudlick, C.J. 2006. "Blind People March for Dr. King." Paper presented at the Society for Disability Studies annual conference, Bethesda, June 2006.

Linton, S. 1998. *Claiming Disability: Knowledge and Identity.* New York: New York University Press.

Massey, D.S. and Lundy, G. 2001. "Use of Black English and Racial Discrimination in Urban Housing Markets: New Methods and Findings." *Urban Affairs Review*, 36(4): 452–269.

Mullings, L. 2005. "Interrogating Racism: Toward an Antiracist Anthropology." *Annual Review of Anthropology*, 34: 667–93.

National Center for Accessible Media. *Mopix Locations.* Accessed July 19, 2006 from http://ncam.wgbh.org/mopix/locations.html.

Oliver, M. 1990. *The Politics of Disablement: A Sociological Approach*. London: Macmillan.

Packer, J. and Kirchner, C. 1997. *Who's Watching: A Profile of the Blind and Visually Impaired Audience for Television and Video*. American Foundation for the Blind; 11 Penn Plaza, Suite 300, New York, NY 10001; www.afb.org.

Piety, P. 2004. "The Language System of Audio Description: An Investigation as a Discursive Process." *Journal of Visual Impairment and Blindness* (*JVIB*), 98(8): 453–69.

Smith, M.M. 2006a. *How Race Is Made: Slavery, Segregation, And The Senses*. Chapel Hill: The University of North Carolina Press.

——. 2006b. "Looking Blindly for Terrorists." *The State* (August 2). Accessed August 16, 2006 from http://www.thestate.com/mld/state/news/opinion/15176961.htm.

Regimes of Vision and Products of Color

Charlene Elliott

Charlene Elliott is an assistant professor in the School of Journalism and Communication, Carleton University. Her research focuses on sensorial communication, color communication, intellectual property law and the formation and maintenance of taste cultures. She is currently leading a research project on the marketing of foods to children. Charlene_Elliott@carleton.ca.

ABSTRACT This article argues in favor of opening up media studies and visual studies to a new line of sensory inquiry – namely, embracing color as a powerful and pertinent mode of communication. It probes the contemporary state of color products and/or products of color through three interconnected categories (that is, color as expression of identity or quality; color as mark of individuality and color as cosmetic) to reveal not only the complex interplay between "signature" and "shock" hues, but also the implications for color codification – and for color communication as a whole.

KEYWORDS: color, visual studies/visual culture, product marketing, color communication, sensory communication

What is at stake, first of all, is an adventure of vision.

(Derrida, *Writing and Difference*)

The inaugural issue of the *Journal of Visual Culture* has Mark Poster articulating a new direction for visual studies: "Visual studies, I propose, is most productively conceived as media studies" (2002: 67). Poster justifies this proposition by pointing to today's vast spread of information machines and a resulting cultural landscape marked by "the digitization of text, sound and image" (2002: 69). What distinguishes our visual regime and separates it from "our ancestors in the Middle Ages" is that "we employ information machines to generate images and, as Virilio argues, to see" (2002: 68).

Poster rightly observes the impact of information machines on contemporary visual culture but perhaps magnifies their import as *the* distinguishing tag of modern society. Other differences exist between the visual regime of today and that of yesterday, and I would like to suggest that beyond the integration of sound, text and image there is a shift in the *deployment* of the visual – our "seeables" have a different gloss. It is not true, as Mirzoeff argues in *An Introduction to Visual Culture* (1999), that "human experience is now more visual and visualized than ever before" (do we use our eyes more than our ancestors did?);[1] rather, the domains of visuality are more open and pliable. This is amply illustrated in the world of color where hue is being newly bent and reworked and becomes the object of a playful bricolage – this, despite the variegated attempts at its codification by industry, corporations and trademark regulations.

So when Poster contends that "the study of visual culture is best serviced by being recast into media studies," we should pay heed, but only if there is a concurrent recasting of media studies itself, one that recognizes "media" as properly configured within the realm of the physical senses. "Media" can be both wired *and non-wired*. (Color, for example, is a kind of media, and is also an extremely powerful communicator which is rarely given its full due in the realm of visual culture.) With media reunderstood, we can take a second look at visual culture to observe intellectual historian Martin Jay's nod, in "Visual Culture and its Vicissitudes" (2002), toward its democratic impulse. This democratization entails: "the growing willingness to take seriously as objects of scholarly inquiry all manifestations of our visual environment and experience, not only those that were deliberately created for aesthetic effects or have been reinterpreted in formalist terms" (Jay 2002: 88). To properly study images, Jay argues, it proves "necessary to focus on how they work and what they do, rather than move past them too quickly to the ideas they represent or the reality they purport to depict" (2002: 88). Technologies of visual production and dissemination are acknowledged by Jay but for him, unlike Poster, visual studies do not have to be contained within the electric fence of information technology.

The starting point for this analysis, then, hides in the spaces of James Elkins's critique of the prevailing definition of visual studies, in which: "visual studies is predominantly about film, photography, advertising, video and the internet. It is predominately not about painting, sculpture or architecture, and it is rarely about any media before 1950 except early film and photography" (2002: 94).

Predominant preoccupations clearly have spaces, and therefore do not preclude the study of peripheral objects, such as the painting *upon* advertising, or the recognition of unusual advertising forms – such as color as a product signifier. This opens the door to considering color communication (and its codification) from an intriguing angle – one that probes the *application* of color on products and asks how it works to both constrain and expand color's repertoire of meanings. So when I argue the domain of visuality is more open and proclaim a shift in the deployment of the visual it is with color squarely in mind. As this article evinces, visual "openness" to color (particularly in the product arena) translates into a willingness to transgress accepted protocols of color use, while a coordinate shift in the deployment of visuality results in a new expression of cultural coloration. Yet in tracing the application of color on products one finds that visual deployments of color "play" appear in the most surprising of places. Particularly surprising is that "shock" hues often debut through the doors of the very businesses that claim ownership of a completely different "signature" color.

Before embarking on this probe into color, it is important to note the following: this particular focus on color and commercial products is merely one aspect of color's communicative power. Color, as a vibrant part of visual culture, communicates in various ways within our contemporary political, legal and symbolic environment. But it does not communicate freely; it is generally both constrained and mediated by social, legal and/or commercial actors. Color is the source of numerous trademark debates and can sit at the core of social movements, communication networks and even networks of power (see Elliott 2003, 2003a, 2005, 2007,). Yet the analysis that follows focuses *specifically* on commercial applications of color and its communicative use in today's marketplace. This focus on commercialization provides a means through which to probe color codification and its broader place in culture. Only this will allow for the disclosed presence of color; or, stated differently, only this will permit us to answer Martin Jay's (earlier noted) questions in light of color images by focusing on "how they work and what they do" instead of dismissing color as an unproblematic element of commercial culture.

Color saturates commercial culture. Glossy magazines, bright packaging and flashy billboards; colored malls and cars and computers and cell phones and clothing – the visual cacophony of Times Square has spread, in various degrees, beyond New York. Color's popularity is expressed from the outer reaches of the cosmos right down to the ground, in headlines trumpeting that astronomers from The Johns Hopkins University (using the "cosmic spectrum") have calculated the color of the universe and in the quiet buzz surrounding Rutgers University's Center for Turfgrass Science, where scientists toy with the idea of marketing orange or red grass made possible through gene manipulation (Spears 2002: A12).[2]

Perhaps this explosion of color comprises a twenty-first-century expression of "ocular madness" – a description Jay used to characterize the undercurrent running beneath Cartesian perspectivalism, the subordinate (and largely overlooked) Baroque scopic regime of modernity. In this regime, the open and pliable nature of visuality (which typifies today's society) triumphs. Extinguish fears of rampant ahistoricism here for, as Jay notes, it is possible to see the baroque "as a permanent if often repressed, visual possibility throughout the modern era" (Jay 1988: 16). This visual possibility strongly relates to conceptions of postmodernity. The baroque scopic regime is "painterly," "multiple, and open," and can be further understood (as per the writings of French philosopher Christine Buci-Glucksmann) as a visual experience "celebrating the dazzling, disorienting, ecstatic surplus of images" (1988: 16).[3] Indeed, it is the postmodern ocular madness of color to which we now turn in *our* culture of dazzling and surfeit images. Spotlighting the surplus of (commercial) color images for their implications, the analysis also suggests how chroma-ocular "madness" shifts our understanding of contemporary communication.

In reviewing the literature on color as well as its commercial use, I propose that color products, and/or products of color, can be understood in three interconnected categories: (a) color as expression of identity or quality, (b) color as mark of individuality and (c) color as cosmetic. All of these categories come bound with a separate set of (often tricky) implications for understanding the role of the senses when it comes to color codification – and to color communication as a whole.

Color as Expression of Identity or Quality

In the product world, this plays out most obviously in the large trademark brands: Coca Cola red and Pepsi blue, Barbie pink and John Deere green – or the signature blue of Tiffany's boxes, used since 1836. Air Canada's Zip airlines colored the runways in September 2002 with its bold palette of blue, fuchsia, orange and green planes. Fruit-flavored iMacs (in blueberry, strawberry, grape, lime and tangerine) stole center stage in 1998 to transform the Apple computer into an aesthetic and tasty digital decor. Nokia, the Finnish telecommunications titan, enjoyed similar distinction by offering the first colored cell phones in 1992. And Orange, part of the France Telecom Group, has trademarked Pantone 23 (orange) in the UK for its exclusive use in the arena of telephones and telecommunications. This is bolstered by its colorful yet simple slogan "The future's bright. The future's Orange."

Hues such as these function to offset particular brands, with tangerine becoming part of the iMac identity and Orange absorbed into telecommunications. Colorful examples like these abound. Consider, for instance, the beverage industry in which color extends far beyond tinting cans red for Coca-cola and blue for Pepsi. Wolf Blass, the internationally renowned Australian wine vintner, has made hue so integral that it actually names wine by color code. Customers simply request Yellow label or Red label – or Green, Brown, Gray or Black label – thus subordinating the all-important varietal to Wolf Blass' "colored" vintages. Or consider Starbucks, which feels its signature green expresses the company so exclusively that it threatened legal action against an independent coffeehouse serving coffee in green cups (McLeod 2001: x). Even liquids can be tinted to express a particular product identity, as per the launch of Code Red Mountain Dew in 2001 or, in 2002, Sobe's *Mr. Green*, Dr Pepper's *Red Fusion* and Pepsico's *Pepsi Blue*, a berry-flavored beverage that is swimming-pool blue.

Quality is also expressed by color, and is perfectly illustrated in the marketing of food. White bread tinted brown is perceived as more healthy while red apples command the highest market price. Oranges with green peels, which can be fully ripe, are degreened with ethylene gas to create a marketable orange color. Myriad scientific studies substantiate the premise that color influences the perception of consumables. Color can alter a food or beverage's perceived flavor, sweetness, intensity, odor or acceptance (Bayarri et al. 2001; Garber et al. 2000; Zellner and Whitten 1999; Strugnell, 1997; Chan and Kane-Martinelli 1997; Oram et al. 1995; Stillman 1993); it can make cherry-flavored drinks taste like orange (Philipsen et al. 1995); and can alter the olfactory judgments of wine tasters (Morrot et al. 2001). Color can make people like yogurt better (Norton and Johnson 1987) or influence the pleasantness of a chocolate's taste (Rolls, Rowe and Rolls 1982).

Perhaps color's power to influence stems partly from its *associative value* (Kandinsky 1947), such as linking red with blood or, in the case of food, associating brown with chocolate. Perhaps, too, this associative value explains the dismal failure of Crystal Pepsi and Miller-Clear beer, two clear beverages that were fundamentally at odds with the visual product *quality* of both cola/caffeine and ale. Indeed, color's associative value or color/quality function also sits at the heart of a long-standing regulatory dispute in over the color of margarine. Canada's province of Quebec is the only place in the world to still ban colored margarine (with the objective of protecting its dairy farmers, who would purportedly lose jobs if consumers could not tell the difference between margarine and butter)

Color as a Mark of Individuality
Categorizing color as *a mark of individuality* brings to mind the 1980s craze of "having your colors done," a complex process of fabric draping and subsequent declarations of the customer-in-question's season, ideal lipstick shade and appropriate fashion hues, as well as the grave determination as to whether she could ever again be permitted to wear black. But color's individual tailoring exists in more subtle variants. Color can be seen to express *character,* a person's identity, personal characteristics, values and interests, as Gunther Kress and Theo van Leeuwen observe by referring to various "expert" discourses surrounding home decoration in "Colour as a Semiotic Mode: Notes for a Grammar of Colour." Quoting from the color therapy book *The Power of Colour to Heal the Environment* (among other sources) Kress and van Leeuwen highlight how "experts" articulate the direct relationship between a home's entrance hall and its owner(s) character or identity:

> A yellow entrance hall usually indicates a person who has ideas and a wide field of interests. A home belonging to an academic would probably contain a distinctive shade of yellow as this colour is associated with the intellect, ideas and a searching mind... A blue entrance hall indicates a place in which people have strong opinions – there could be a tendency to appear aloof as they can be absorbed too much in their own world. (Lacy, cited in Kress and van Leeuwen 2002: 358)

Color's power to reflect personal identity is also suggested in quirky products designed not to paint the environment, but to *record* it. Polaroid's i-Zone Color Changing Instant Camera, for example, takes inspiration from the mood rings popular in the 1960s and changes color based on an individual's body heat. The camera, like the entrance hall, suggests personal identity based on surface representations, which is reinforced by Polaroid's press release that claims users of the color-changing technology "have an individualized experience with the camera each time they point and click." Presumably this "individualized experience" transforms a mass-produced, marketed item into a personal sign; it certainly gives new meaning to John Berger's (1972) claim that *to see is to own,* for now the selection and framing of objects though the camera lens is complemented by a personal expression that *others* (like those in front of the camera) can see. Still, the "ownership" resides squarely in the hands of the camera holder, who alone (through body heat) determines what color the others see.

Consumers' apparent determining power over color also plays out in marketing campaigns geared to emphasize people's role in choosing the colors in our world. M&M's Global Color Vote™, launched by Masterfoods USA in March 2002, provides a perfect illustration of this: "Residents from every region of the world will be eligible to vote" for the newest M&M color "by logging on to www.mms.com", claims the company's press release. Despite its less-than-democratic voting procedures which made eligibility contingent upon internet accessibility, Masterfoods proudly announced on June 19, 2002 that "the world" chose purple (over pink and aqua) as M&M's newest color. What does this mean to color communication? Firstly, it underpins Elfriede Fursich and Elli Roushanzamir's *commodification model of communication* which, in light of the economic impact and cultural expansion of corporations, views "communication as always commmodified" (2001: 392). Under this commodification model, the audience is positioned as a consumer *not* a citizen, and public spaces become increasingly commercialized "while seemingly maintaining a public/democratic image and functions" (2001: 393). With the M&M Global Color Vote™, democratic action is reduced to a literal shell. Meaningful choice here equates to selecting *one* color in a handful of candies, a color that will scatter, thanks to the international reach of Masterfoods, through public space with the seeming benison of the global populace. This illusion of choice is bolstered by the marketing of M&M's candy kaleidoscope of colors. The brown-coated chocolate pellets introduced to US consumers in 1941 splintered into brown, red, green and yellow in 1960, and, by 1996, the twenty-one brightly colored M&Ms available allowed consumers to create "their own personalized color blends to add their unique touch of color to every special occasion" (http://global.mms.com). This touch differs from the physical alteration witnessed with Polaroid's i-Zone, but is nonetheless presented as a form of participatory action. Consumers can use M&M's Colorworks Candies to create their team, school or corporate colors, to match wedding colors or to celebrate holidays. Equally, consumers are informed that purchasing M&Ms in particular color schemes can equate to nothing short of a patriotic act: Americans can "celebrate the freedom and independence" of the fourth of July by purchasing, for example, Stars & Stripes M&M colors (in red, white and blue) (www.colorworks.com). Owning this colored mix, like painting an entrance hall a particular shade, apparently demonstrates personal character traits – in this case it allows consumers to "show off [their] pride." Masterfoods also prods consumers to display compassion through colored candy purchases, as in the initiative spearheaded to raise money for the American Red Cross: "Order a set of Red, White and Blue 'M&M's'® packs and 'M&M's'® Brand will donate 100% of product sales price to the American Red Cross Disaster Relief Fund. It's one way you can help those in need" (www.colorworks.com). Here, help comes *not* from candy but from its particular color – apparently the palette of compassion exists solely in red, white and blue.

Color as Cosmetic

In many respects, color's *cosmetic* nature embraces the previous categories whereby hue marks identity, quality or individuality. Color categories bleed together, for the qualities or particular identity suggested by color is tightly bound with ideas of costuming. Even color's etymology reveals its relationship with the costume or cosmetic: "the Latin *colorem* is related to *celare,* to hide or conceal," although it originally meant a covering; "in Middle English 'to color' is to embellish or adorn, to disguise, to render specious or plausible, to misrepresent" (Batchelor 2000: 52). Linguistic science thus suggests we approach the cosmetic of color with caution – for what deceptions or dangers may hide beneath the bright packaging?

David Batchelor's *Chromophobia* (2000) argues that the "cosmetic" is one primary lens through which Western culture views, and consistently devalues, color. To Batchelor, "if the cosmetic is essentially anything, it is essentially visible ... essentially visible, essentially superficial and thinner than the skin onto which it is applied. Cosmetics adorn, embellish, supplement" (2000: 52). In short, the cosmetic – frivolous and superficial as it may be – decorates our world. It brightens the visual culture Poster wants to move into media studies and adds the dazzle to the "ecstatic surplus of images" characterizing our postmodern "baroque scopic regime."[4] And in the realm of commodity culture, color can provide the spectacle that seizes consumer attention. Let's sidestep the obvious examples of the way Coca-Cola red encases its brown liquid – or saturates the signage of developed and developing countries alike. Trademark colors such as these can be viewed as color "regularities," signs that, according to Kress and van Leeuwen, "arise from the interests of the sign makers" and are "not at all arbitrary or anarchic" (2002: 345). Instead of discussing a typical line-up of color's cosmetic applications, I would like to focus instead *on* the arbitrary or anarchic, on the more remarkable cosmetic applications in the product world, applications that emphasize the "essentially visible" nature of color and its power to adorn. "Remarkable" cosmetic applications, it is important to note, span a range of product categories, and the selection of products highlighted is in many ways as frivolous as the colors that supplement them: I have chosen products that have caught my eye, ones that evince an openness to color application and display the relative plasticity of color in an environment that is equally preoccupied with controlling it.

Batchelor's notion of the cosmetic is abundantly displayed in the world of food, where the "essentially visible and superficial" (2000: 52) is a virtual creed and embellishments by color often efface the product being adorned. *Essentially visible* today are a host of pointedly decorated items: Heinz's EZ Squirt Blastin' Green and Funky Purple and Stellar Blue Ketchup, Dr Pepper's Red Fusion, Pepperidge Farm's rainbow colored Goldfish, Kraft's Blue's Clues

Macaroni and Cheese (with blue-colored paw prints) and Mott's Blue's Clues Berry Flavored Apple Sauce – tinted an appetizing "theme-park-water-ride" blue. Cereals, of course, come all colors of the rainbow: beyond Rainbow Rice Krispies and the artificial glare of Fruit Loops are Kellogg's vibrant green Apple Jacks, green and purple Buzz Blasts and the multi-colored Mickey's Magix, which "magically" turns milk pastel blue. Heralding this "blue magic" theme in 2000 was Nabisco's limited edition Oreo Magic Dunkers that, when dunked in milk, also turned it blue. Less interactive (but also blue) are Kellogg's Frosted Wild MagicBurst blue raspberry striped Pop Tarts. Or, for the very adventurous, there are mystery-colored consumables, including Kool-Aid Magic Twists Switchin' Secret®, a drink mix that "turns into a secret color and flavor" (Kraft 2002), or Frito Lay's Mystery Colorz Snack Cheetos which, while still neon orange, turn the venturous consumer's tongue either blue or green. Herr's pink Changing Cheddar Magic Popcorn also promises a green tongue. Heinz, too, entered the mystery world in 2002 with its suspenseful EZ Squirt Mystery Color ketchup, in which the bottle veils the condiment inside – colored either Passion Pink, Awesome Orange or Totally Teal.

What to make of this colorful array of consumables? Obviously, "electric blue" fries grab attention, but there is a communicative problem that rests behind the products that present – and the marketing that trumpets – the incongruity of startling food colors. For *marketing communication* purposes, novel colors can mean increased sales: the strategy is "to celebrate the very incongruity of a novel food color, to announce to the consumer that its novelty is there to surprise and delight and the proper response is to have fun and enjoy it" (Garber et al. 2000: 68), and this strategy seems prudent in an era of communicative abundance. It provides another means of making a product stand out from the hundreds of competing products vying for the consumer's attention. But these incongruous hues raise a different set of issues for *communication*, ones that pertain to the excess of images and their impact, the bending of color communication and the "deception" of ornament. If these startling colors make products stand out, if they spark delight in the consumer, they equally speak to a movement within the broader culture. And this movement shows considerable power accorded to color. Consider Alexander Garcia Duttmann's brief expository on visual culture in light of hue: Duttmann notes that among other things, visual culture means that "a culture is based on images rather than on concepts, or that images have become predominant within a particular culture and have replaced words" (2002: 101). With the blue food craze – blue fries, applesauce, cola, margarine and macaroni and cheese – *color* speaks volumes. Rhetorical claims of *New and Improved!* or *Even Better!* can recede since the material substance assumes and absorbs (modernity's) "message" of the new. Passion Pink ketchup and Shocking Pink margarine have no need for *words* about their novelty for it spills from their squeeze bottles and chatters back from plate.

Derrida's "adventure of vision" (noted in the introduction of this paper) thus begins. For there *is* an adventure promised by color here, an adventure that begins with the deliberate breaking of color's accepted code. Color codification is unquestionably present, peering out from behind the camouflage of Awesome Orange Heinz to see if we get the joke. The play or delight experienced comes from the knowledge that ketchup is not *supposed* to be orange, that the visual representation is itself an image, an artifice and a cosmetic. Clearly many bizarrely tinted foods are targeted at children, where the delight is reserved for the youngsters and the joke is on the parents who may not find the pointedly artificial foodstuffs particularly appetizing. But the adventure requires more than the acknowledgement that businesses spend roughly $10 billion each year trying to capture the "tastes" of children (Mishra 2005): it has first to reveal its magic and then ponder, "How did we get here?" and "What does it mean?"

Today's "magic of color" is far removed from Hegel's discussion in his *Aesthetics* on "the magic of color and the secrets of its spell" (cited in Riley 1995: 23). Hegel's work, addressing the philosophy of beauty and the power of color, finds that color's "magic" inheres in its ability to create in paintings the sensation of spatial relations, shape, distance, boundaries and contours. Its magic further springs from a system that creates harmony by "embracing all the hues of the spectrum in one translucent effect" and that draws from a palette where all tones are equal in priority (Riley 1995: 24). Hegel's *magician* is the artist who handles color in such a manner that the "substance and spirit of objects" (Hegel 1975: 848) evaporates.

> The magic consists in so handling all the colors that what is produced is an inherently objectless play of pure appearance which forms the extreme soaring pinnacle of coloring, a fusion of colors, a shining of reflections upon one another which become so fine, so fleeting, so expressive of the soul that they begin to pass over into the sphere of music.... Owing to this ideality, this fusion, this hither and thither of reflections and sheens of color, this mutability and fluidity of transitions, there is spread over the whole, with the clarity, the brilliance, the depth, the smooth and luscious lighting of colors, a pure appearance of animation; and this is what constitutes the magic of coloring and is properly due to the spirit of the artist who is the magician. (Hegel 1975: 848)

With commercial color "magic," Hegel's "objectless play of pure appearance" is utterly bent so that the new end becomes the *play of pure appearance of objects*. Its magic is not to create the illusion of harmony as Hegel would like, but to revel in the discordant, to transform ketchup from the common to the curious. Color's mutability and fluid transitions created by the hands of an artistic genius, which Hegel so appreciated, is equally transformed in today's commercial marketplace: enter here Kool-Aid Magic Twists, an "interactive" drink mix that, according to Kraft's tagline, "Changes colors right before your mouth!" Kool-Aid's Changin' Cherry is a green powder that turns blue (but tastes like cherry) while Grape Illusion's gold powder turns red (but tastes like grape). Here the "fluid" transitions are literal and ironic, the "mutability" a game; the magic is not the artistic creation of a genius, but the stained alchemy that promises blue milk out of Oreo Magic Dunkers and Mickey's Magix, and blue tongues out of Mystery Cheetos. As with the Global M&M vote, the participatory action required for this alchemy is nothing more than a shell or cosmetic. Hegel's magician of color *creates* the masterpiece, brings it into being, infuses it with spirit; today's magician adds water, stirs and waits to see what happens. Given this, colored products are more in keeping with Batchelor's claim that "figuratively, color has always meant the less-than-true and the not-quite-real." Not-quite-real, tellingly, is another way to describe the sleight-of-hand that can also parade as magic.

Deception ... or Disclosure?

Here we must give pause to ask if the adventure is one of deception. Is there some striking disclosure to be found in *this* excess of color, in its deliberate breaking of the color code and in its promise of magic? According to Batchelor's survey of Western civilization's attitude toward color since antiquity many voices in philosophy, art, art history and literature would say "no." Aristotle called color *pharmakon* – a drug (Batchelor 2000: 31) – and art critic Charles Blanc warned that an excess of color over design in painting would lead to destruction: "it will fall through color just as mankind fell through Eve" (Blanc, quoted in Riley 1995: 6). Le Corbusier considered color in architecture a "modern form of degeneration" (Batchelor 2000: 45) and Batchelor sums up Western culture's prevailing attitudes with the claim that

> colour, then, is arbitrary and unreal: mere make-up. But while it may be superficial, that is not quite the same as it being trivial, for cosmetic colour is also always less than honest. There is an ambiguity in make-up; cosmetics can often confuse, cast doubt, mask or manipulate; they can produce illusions or deceptions – and this makes them sound more than a little like drugs. (2000: 52)

Duplicity, it seems, rests at the core of the colored world. Batchelor continues, arguing that part of the problem resides in the "make-up" of color:

> If surface veils depth, if appearance masks essence, then make-up masks a mask, veils a veil, disguises a disguise.

It is not simply a deception; it is a double deception. It is a surface on a surface, and thus even farther from substance than "true" appearance. How things appear is one thing; how things appear to appear is another. Colour is a double illusion, a double deception. (2000: 54)

This sounds an awful lot like hyperbolic word play, especially in view of the novelty-hued products whose very appeal stems from the utter surface-ness of the surface. Ostensibly, Ore-Ida's fries are more appealing because we *know* they are disguised in "electric" blue – the fact that we are *not* deceived makes them special.[5] So where is the deception? Deception intuitively must reside in the coloring that *pretends* to be real, the green oranges gassed until they are orange, the yellow-tinted margarine that impersonates butter. But colorful hue can hide something else, something media critics like Marcel O'Gorman find altogether distressing: emasculation. O'Gorman looks at the colorful shells and custom desktops of computers, identifying the "digital peacocking" of the computer fashion scene as "the site of disempowerment, programmed ignorance, and packaged identity formation" (2000: para. 1). The problem for O'Gorman is that the pretty colors and desktops of the iMac (for example) distract consumers from the important issue of understanding *how* the machine works – we should know how to *control* the computer, he argues, not display it as an accessory! Tinted computers become "personal style-voguish signifiers of well being" and the aesthetic fillips ultimately anesthetize: "as the desktop computer becomes more simple to use and more attractive to behold, the user is unwittingly faced with an increasing loss of power and control over the machine" (2000: para. 1). Dire consequences will result from this colorful seduction O'Gorman warns. Users, increasingly reliant on the pretty corporate fashion machines delivering their information, fail to realize the extent to which they are disempowered *and also deceived* by the corporate giants that create aesthetic hardware and software, but *also* filter, shape and ultimately control information. Here, where we do not recognize the disguise, Batchelor's commentary on double deception makes more sense.

The deception also makes sense when the colors are presented as if a form of empowerment – casting electronic votes on the next M&M shell color, changing gold powder into red drink – for this is an empowerment of trifles. This manipulation of the visual media of color (along with O'Gorman's histrionic, if not absurd, concerns about digital peacocking) inevitably brings us full circle, back to the beginning of this paper and to Poster's analysis of visual culture as media culture, because mass mediation *does* occur, although it is not solely in terms of information machines. Poster (2002) observes that media are fundamentally changing, expanding and interacting with each other in unpredictable ways (i.e., the internet absorbing radio, film and television) – and when I suggest that his observations equally apply to the media of color (whose application is also changing, expanding and interacting "unpredictably" with other media), my intent is not to pervert or radically decontextualize his work but to point to a similarity between these visual cultures, wired and non-wired. As per the digital world, there is an "open content" to commercial color, a material transformation *suggested* (and also perceived) by the changing of Heinz red to pink, purple, green, orange or teal. This "content" is mediated by those who choose the colors or create the cosmetic, and curiously, a new product relationship is promised to the consumer with the addition of each new hue.

In winding up this journey on "regimes of vision and products of color," Derrida's introductory quote has great meaning, for "what is at stake, after all, is an adventure of vision." But the adventure still needs to make sense from a communication perspective: it cannot end without first responding to those questions posed earlier of "How did we get here?" and "What does it mean?"

Answering the first query requires a look at our current visual culture, one characterized by myriad forms of media(ted) messages and an incredible surplus of images – a culture of communicative abundance. Arthur Kroker claims that modern society is no longer characterized by the disembodied eye:

> It is the age of the bored eye: the eye which flits from situation to situation, from scene to scene, from image to image, from ad to ad, with a restlessness and high-pitched consumptive appetite that can never really ever be satisfied. The bored eye ... demands novelty. It loves junk images. It turns recombinant when fed straight narratives. It has ocular appetites that demand satisfaction. (2002)

Kroker's "bored eye" contains the same restlessness of Jay's "ocular madness." This eye delights in purple Heinz then just as quickly demands passion pink, it relishes bending the color code simply for the sake of bending it. We have reached this stage of boredom, claims Kroker, primarily because of digital technology, which causes the disappearance of the image into virtuality, and because of the velocity and intensity of image proliferation. The bored eye exists, Kroker says, because virtuality has triumphed and our culture has lost faith in representability. It is proper to acknowledge Kroker's explanations for the bored eye, even though they revolve around digital culture and thus really do not concern us here. Digitality is merely *part* of our culture, it does not wholly define or explain it. And I must disagree with Kroker in part: we have not lost faith in representability – not the representability of color, at least – for its role in signaling product identity, quality and individuality is strongly heeded. "Loss of faith" is not quite right in the understanding of pointedly cosmetic products either; in opening up material content to radical colors our society is simply no longer taking the color representation *seriously* (i.e., margarine does not *have* to be yellow). The color code is still important – but important precisely so it can be broken.

If communicative abundance and the bored eye explain our culture's readiness for chroma-ocular madness then what are the implications of this phenomenon? In one sense, color has clearly been hijacked, subverted by the very corporations that seek to codify hues for particular ends. This hijacking of color is *not* attempted for the purposes of *détournement*, for revealing the utter artificiality of particular products (as the Situationists might have done) by creating its vivid parody. Rather, the colorful diversion occurs to consolidate the product's power, to move it into centre stage.

Color codification is still at play, although now with a theatrics and a series of tinted promises: promises of marking individuality, participatory action and patriotic display; promises of fun, delight and magic; promises of artistry and colorful adventure. These are surface promises, cosmetic ones, ones that occur within a commodification model as part of a large corporate network in which *sales* stand as the ultimate end of a communicative act. Remarkably, many of these promises inhere *in the colors themselves* and their particular application, and in the suggestion that the associative quality assigned to particular hues can be delightfully bent. Yet this product costuming, by its capacity to distract, can be viewed as deceptive (i.e., Batchelor) or even destructive (O'Gorman).

Thankfully, a broader perspective exists, one that moves beyond the product world. Excess in commercial color use suggests that *despite* the existence of codification, color has limitless applications. We can either lament its artificiality or revel in its plasticity; and despite the general hollowness of the marketed promises within our colored product world, a spontaneity remains. The commercial origin of this particular color spontaneity robs it of authenticity, yet the message is legitimate: the commonness of color, its excess, does not necessitate that it fade from view. From a communication perspective, marketing shock hues is like deliberately introducing noise into a network and then asking people to listen to the static: it's jarring, distracting and often a little more than irritating – but it prompts one to look at the communication system more closely to see what is going on. This scrutiny reveals a visual culture with *more* than information machines comprising its media forms and with a strangeness that suggests color's pure potential to awe.

Acknowledgements
The author would like to thank the reviewers of this piece for their thoughtful commentary.

Notes
1. This observation is drawn from Poster's (2002) article, which respectfully challenges Mirzoeff's claim.

2. The color of the universe was calculated by charting data from the Australian 2df Galaxy Redshift Survey, which analyzes over 200,000 galaxies situated two to three billion light years from earth. Combining these galaxies into the "Cosmic Spectrum," Karl Glazebrook and Ivan Baldry calculated the color that would be seen if the energy from all those 200,000 galaxies and their corresponding light wavelengths focused on one point (see Recer 2002 and McKeen 2002).
3. The periodization of scopic regimes obviously requires some elaboration: Jay's article titled "Scopic Regimes of Modernity" observes that, while the modern era has been dominated by the sense of sight, *competing* scopic regimes exist – visuality is contested terrain. Jay thus sketches out three main "visual subcultures" in modernity: *Cartesian perspectivalism* (which flourished in the Renaissance and is presented as the dominant – and often the sole – visual model of modernity); *the art of describing* (characteristic of seventeenth-century Dutch painting, and defined by arbitrary frames and the interest in depicting a fragmentary world); and *the baroque* (a style characterized by ocular madness). Jay claims that "although it may be prudent to confine the baroque largely to the seventeenth century and link it with the Catholic Counter Reformation or the manipulation of popular culture by the newly ascendant absolutist state – *it may also be possible to see it as a permanent, if often repressed, visual possibility throughout the entire modern era*" (1988: 16). Jay goes on to affirm that "if one had to single out the scopic regime that has finally come into its own in our own time, it would be the 'madness of vision' identified with the baroque" (1988: 19).
4. As per the discussion on Jay presented earlier in this article.
5. This relates to Kress and Van Leeuwen's (earlier noted) observation on the regularities of color use. Kress and Van Leeuwen's article on the semiotics of color also explains that, as a grammar, color's regularities can be contravened (2002: 346). In this case, the existence of blue fries or blue macaroni would comprise a contravention of color's regularity, an "ungrammatical" use of the semiotic resource.

References

Batchelor, D. 2000. *Chromophobia*. London: Reaktion Books.

Bayarri, S., Calvo, C., Costell, E. and Duran, L. 2001. "Influence of Color on Perception of Sweetness and Fruit Flavor of Fruit Drinks." *Food Science and Technology International*, 7(5): 399–404.

Berger, J. 1972. *Ways of Seeing*. London: British Broadcasting Corporation.

Chan, M.M., and Martinelli, C. 1997. "The Effect of Color on Perceived Flavor Intensity and Acceptance of Foods by Young Adults and Elderly Adults," *Journal of the American Dietetic Association*, 97(6): 657–9.

Derrida, J. 1978. *Writing and Difference*. Chicago: University of Chicago Press.

Duttmann, A.G. 2002. "The ABC of Visual Culture, or a New Decadence of Illiteracy." *Journal of Visual Culture*, 1(1): 101–3.

Elkins, J. 2002. "Preface to the Book: A Skeptical Introduction to Visual Culture." *Journal of Visual Culture*, 1(1): 93–9.

Elliott, C. 2003. "Colour Codification: Law, Culture and the Hue of Communication." *Journal for Cultural Research*, 7(3): 297–319.

——. 2003a. "Crayoning Culture: The 'Colour Elite' and the Commercial Nature of Colour Standardization." *Canadian Review of American Studies*, 33(1): 37–59.

——. 2005. "Colour: Law and the Sensory Scan." *M/C Journal*, 8(4). Available online: http://journal.media-culture.org.au/0508/06-elliott.php.

——. n.d. "Code Pink!: On Colour (and Contention) in Public Space." *Canadian Journal of Communication*, 31(3). Forthcoming.

Fursich, E. and Lester Roushanzamir, E.P. 2001. "Corporate Expansion, Textual Expansion: Commodification Model of Communication." *Journal of Communication Inquiry*, 25(4): 375–95.

Garber, L.L., Hyatt, E.M. and Starr, R.G. 2000. "The Effects of Food Color on Perceived Flavour." *Journal of Marketing Theory and Practice*, 8(4): 59–72.

Hegel, G.W.F. [1903] 1975. *Aesthetics: Lectures on Fine Art*. Translated by T. M. Knox. 2 vols. Oxford: Oxford University Press.

Jay, M. 1988. "Scopic Regimes of Modernity." In H. Foster (ed.), *Vision and Visuality*. Seattle: Bay Press: 3 – 27.

——. 2002. "That Visual Turn: The Advent of Visual Culture." *Journal of Visual Culture*, 1(1): 87–92. [Interview with M. Smith.]

Kandinsky, W. [1912] 1947. *Concerning the Spiritual in Art*. New York: Wittenborn.

Kraft .2002. Kool-Aid® Magic Twists Flavors. http://www.kraftfoods.com/kool-aid/2001/ka_flavor_switchin_secret.html (accessed December 15, 2002).

Kress, G. and T. van Leeuwen. 2002. "Colour as a Semiotic Mode: Notes for a Grammar of Colour." *Visual Communication*, 1(3): 343 – 68.

Kroker, A. 2002. "The Image Matrix." *CTheory*, 25(1 – 2). Available online: http://www.ctheory.net.

McKeen, S. 2002. "Color our Universe Pale Aquamarine". *Edmonton Journal* (January 11), p. A1.

McLeod, K. 2001. *Owning Culture: Authorship, Ownership and Intellectual Property Law*. New York: Peter Lang Publishers.

Mirzoeff, N. 1999. *An Introduction to Visual Culture*. New York: Routledge.

Mishra, R. 2005. April 18. "Push Grows to Limit Food Ads to Children." *The Boston Globe*.

Morrot, G., Brochet, F. and Debourdieu, D. 2001. "The Color of Odors." *Brain and Language*, 79: 309 – 20.

Norton, W. and Johnson, F.N. 1987. "The Influence of Intensity of Color on Perceived Flavour Characteristics." *Medical Science Research*, 15(5–8): 329–30.

O'Gorman, M. 2000. "You Can't Always Get What You Want: Transparency and Deception on the Computer Fashion Scene." *CTheory*, E094. Available online: www.ctheory.net/text_file?pick=227

Oram, N, Laing, D.G. and Newell, G. 1995. "The Influence of Flavor and Color on Drink Identification by Children and Adults." *Developmental Psychobiology*, 28(4): 239 – 46.

Philipsen, D.H., Clydesdale, F.M. and Stern, P. 1995. "Consumer Age Affects Response to Sensory Characteristics of a Cherry Flavored Beverage." *Journal of Food Science*, 60(2): 364-8.

Poster, M. 2002. "Visual Studies as Media Studies." *Journal of Visual Culture*, 1(1): 67–70.

Recer, P. 2002. "Color Corrected: John Hopkins Researchers Say Universe Much Blander than Before." *Space*. www.space.com (accessed March 23, 2002).

Riley, C.A. 1995. *Color Codes*. London: University Press of New England.

Rolls, B., Rowe, E. and Rolls, E. 1982. "How Sensory Properties of Food Affect Human Feeding Behavior." *Physiology and Behavior*, 29(3): 409–17.

Spears, T. 2002. "Why Settle for Green Grass When it Could be Hot Pink?" *Ottawa Citizen* (May 23) pp. A1, A12.

Stillman, J.A. 1993. "Color Influences Flavor Identification in Fruit-Flavored Beverages." *Journal of Food Science*, 58(4): 810–12.

Strugnall, C. 1997. "Color and its Role in Sweetness Perception." *Appetite*, 28: 85.

Zellner, D.A. and Whitten, L.A. 1999. "The Effect of Color Intensity and Appropriateness on Color-induced Odor Enhancement." *American Journal of Psychology*, 112(4): 585–604.

Slow Living

By Wendy Parkins and Geoffrey Craig

"Highly original, exciting and timely ... there is certainly no other book like it."

Dr. David Bell, Sociology Department, Manchester Metropolitan University

"...a cutting-edge book that raises important questions about modern social movements and globalization."

Carole Counihan, Professor of Anthropology, Millersville University

"An intelligent analysis of the stresses of contemporary society."

The Saturday Guardian

Speed is the essence of the modern era, but our faster, more frenetic lives often trouble us and leave us wondering how we are meant to live in today's world. *Slow Living* **explores the philosophy and politics of 'slowness' as it investigates the growth of Slow Food into a worldwide, 'eco-gastronomic' movement.**

February 2006 • 256pp • 10 b/w illus
ISBN 978 1 84520 160 9 (PB) £16.99 • $29.95
ISBN 978 1 84520 159 3 (HB) £55.00 • $99.95
www.bergpublishers.com

BERG

Sensing Cittàslow: Slow Living and the Constitution of the Sensory City

Sarah Pink

Sarah Pink is Senior Lecturer in Sociology at Loughborough University. Her research focuses on the senses, gender, media, home and, currently, the Slow City movement. Her books include *Women and Bullfighting* (1997), *Doing Visual Ethnography* (2001, 2007), *Home Truths* (2004), *The Future of Visual Anthropology* (2005) and *Visual Interventions* (2007).
http://www.lboro.ac.uk/departments/ss/depstaff/staff/pink.htm

ABSTRACT   In 2004 Aylsham, Norfolk, became Britain's second Cittàslow Town (Slow City). Embedded within the slow living ideology of Cittàslow is the assumption that the "better" life it advocates involves heightened sensory experience and concomitant pleasure. In contrast to contemporary fast life, it wishes that "suitable doses of guaranteed sensual pleasure and slow, long-lasting enjoyment [may] preserve us from the contagion of the multitude who mistake frenzy for efficiency" (*The Slow Food Companion* 2005: 6). In the first part of the paper I analyze how the sensory elements of slow living are represented in the Cittàslow and related Slow Food movement's literature. Then, based on my ethnographic fieldwork centered on Aylsham's Cittàslow events and projects, I examine how the routine and creative sensory practices of the individuals who produce and participate in Cittàslow policies and activities are constitutive of a "sensory city."

KEYWORDS: sensory city, urban anthropology, Cittàslow movement, ethnography

Introduction

In 2004, Aylsham in Norfolk became (after Ludlow in Shropshire) Britain's second Cittàslow Town or "Slow City." Embedded within the slow-living ideology of Cittàslow and the connected movement Slow Food is the assumption that the "better" life it advocates involves heightened sensory experience and concomitant pleasure. In contrast to the fast pace of contemporary life it wishes that:

> suitable doses of guaranteed sensual pleasure and slow, long-lasting enjoyment [may] preserve us from the contagion of the multitude who mistake frenzy for efficiency (*The Slow Food Companion* 2005: 6)

Cittàslow was founded in 1999 in Italy. It now has over fifty member towns (Town Councils, not individuals, become members). Cittàslow UK was established in 2004. To achieve Cittàslow accreditation a town must meet specified criteria concerning its environmental and infrastructure policies, the quality of its urban fabric, its encouragement of local produce, its hospitality and community and the creation of Cittàslow awareness. Cittàslow emphasises local distinctiveness in a context of globalization by focusing on "small realities in a more and more global connected world" (Cittàslow Philosophy as stated on www.cittaslow.net) and seeking to improve the quality of life locally. Cittàslow towns are expected to continue to develop in these areas through organizing and engaging in projects, activities and events that support the Cittàslow philosophy (www.cittaslow.net).

The ideas of the slow living movement strike a chord in recent work in urban design studies. Paul Knox (2005) suggests that the principles of the Cittàslow movement "speak directly to the concepts of 'dwelling' and intersubjectivity that are key to the social construction of place and, therefore, to successful urban design." In architectural and design studies Juhani Pallasmaa (whose writings also resonate more generally with the philosophy of the slow living movement)[1] urges designers to go beyond the idea of the city as a *visible* form (see, for instance, 2005). He suggests that "the city of the gaze passivates the body and the other senses, the alienation of the body again reinforces visibility" (2005: 142–3) and draws from Merleau Ponty to see the city as an embodied experience through which "we mold the mosaic of sensory impressions into a coherent continuum." This process is in itself constitutive of self-identity as the embodied self and the city thus "supplement and mutually define each other" (2005: 144). Pallasmaa's ideas are cogent with interdisciplinary understandings of how self-identities and environments are coproduced and my own work on the mutual constitution of self and home (as domestic interior) as a sensory embodied process (Pink 2004). But, like Joy Malnar and Frank Vodvarka who, writing from a design studies perspective, also insist that an understanding of cities as (multi)sensory domains should inform design practice (see, for example, Malnar and Vodvarka 2004: 266–72), Pallsamaa relies not on sensory ethnographies of how urban (and more generally architectural) environments are experienced, but on literary representations (Italo Calvino's and Rainer Maria Rilke's work, for example, among others).

Social and cultural anthropologists drawing from ethnographic studies of sensory experience, and often also, like Pallasmaa and others, from the work of Merleau Ponty, have also demonstrated that the way people experience their environments is inevitably multisensory. Recent critiques of how "ethnographic and cultural geographic work on senses of place has been dominated by the visualism deeply rooted in the European concept of landscape" (Feld 2005: 182) have led to a focus on how the senses are implicated in such experiences, in social anthropology and cultural geography. Anthropological work in modern Western cultures (e.g. Desjarlais 2005, Pink 2004) and elsewhere (e.g. Feld 2005, Geurts 2002, Desjarlais 2003) has made it clear that sensory experience of a particular type of physical and material environment (be it a forest in Papua New Guinea, a Spanish kitchen or a shelter for the homeless in the USA) is inextricable from the cultural knowledge and everyday practices through which localities are constructed and experienced. Likewise, cultural geographers have recognized the city as a sensory domain (for example, Amin and Thrift 2002: 111–14) and the importance of studying people's sensory practices in cities ethnographically (for instance, Law 2005). David Howes has suggested using the notion of "emplacement" to theorize people's relationships to their environments. He notes how "we usually think of emplacement in terms of our visible and tangible surroundings" (2005: 7–8), and the term has frequently been used to refer to people's relationships to landscape (as, for example, Stewart and Strathern 2003: 1). But as Howes points out, "we relate to and create environments through all of our senses" (2005: 7–8), thus reconceptualizing emplacement to depart from the notion of "embodiment" and suggest "the sensuous interrelationship of body-mind-environment" (2005: 7). We do not, of course, simply passively experience urban environments; rather, as Stephen Feld puts it, "emplacement always implicates the intertwined nature of sensual bodily presence and perceptual engagement" (2005: 181).

We are involved in a continuous process of emplaced engagement with the material, sensory, social and cultural contexts in which we dwell. This can be conceptualized in terms of four forms of engagement which are inextricably intertwined in complex ways. First is what Victor Turner (1986) called "mere experience": *the continuous flow of undefined sensory emplaced experience*. Second is our definition of that experience. By reflecting on "mere experience" we convert it into what Turner (1986) called "an experience" and, for instance, use linguistic metaphors to express this. For example, "the town was buzzing with the farmers market this morning," or, "I felt soft soil underfoot." Through this we create and verbalize or enact culturally specific sensory knowledge about the urban environment. Third is *everyday sensory practice*: our engagement in the everyday routine activities that constitute our self identities in relation to the objects, persons, ideas and intangible elements of the environments with which we interact. Practice is both based on and produces sensory experience and knowledge. Fourth is *sensory creativity*. Sensory creativity is inextricable from sensory practice since it involves engaging in practices that are intended to produce changes in the sensory environment and thus in our experience of it. It assumes, however, departures from routine practice to stress a degree of human agency, intentionality and the ability to *act on* the urban environment. It does not, though, preclude the idea that the sensory and material context of the city also acts on *us*, and as such has a form of agency of its own. This agency, however, like Daniel Miller's (2001) notion of "estate agency" in which the home can limit our potential to act on it, does not refer to the independent power of the city itself. Rather, it reflects how urban design manifests the ideologies adhered to and the agency of town planners, architects, landscape gardeners and others to create urban spaces that can impinge on the agency of local people.

Given the slow living movement's own emphasis on attention to sensory experience, knowledge and practice on the one hand and, on the other, recent attention to the senses in urban design studies and anthropology, Cittàslow is an interesting case study through which to examine the notion of the sensory city and how it is shaped through local people's emplaced engagements with their urban environment. In this article I shall suggest that Cittàslow, through both its literature and through practice, is involved in processes that constitute particular types of urban (sensory) experience. The ideologies that inform the Cittàslow model (in turn derived from the ideals of the Slow Food movement), suggest that a sustainable, "better" and more pleasurable form of urban life may be achieved in two ways. First, through the implementation of design and social policies which fulfill Cittàslow criteria. Second, in adopting the emphasis Slow Food discourse places on working towards the aims of the movement (that is, slowing down globalization, promoting biodiversity and educating others along these lines) which involves engaging in everyday practice in particular ways at a routine, personal, individual level as well as through the production of one-off celebratory events and projects with specific aims (such as transmission of knowledge). The first part of the paper will analyze how the sensory elements of slow living are represented in this literature. The second part of the paper, situated in relation to this literature, will be based on my ethnographic fieldwork in Aylsham.[2] By examining Cittàslow events and projects I examine how the routine and creative sensory practices of the individuals who produce and participate in Cittàslow policies, projects and activities are constitutive of a "sensory city."

The Slow Living Movement
The analysis in the following section is based on existing Slow Food and Cittàslow literature published in print form by the movement's own publishing company, Slow Food Editore, and on-line on its web sites www.slowfood.com and www.cittaslow.net. Slow Food and Cittàslow are inextricably related. A standard version of the history of the Slow Food movement has been recounted in more detail in numerous existing publications (see especially Petrini 2001) including academic works (for instance, Parkins and Craig 2006). Very briefly, its history, with specific reference to the establishment of Slow Food and Cittàslow in Britain is as follows: the Slow Food movement was formed by its current leader, Carlo Petrini, in Italy in 1986, and launched as an international movement in Paris in 1989 (Petrini 2001, Parkins 2004). It now has over 80,000 members internationally and the Slow Food UK office was set up in the English town of Ludlow, in 2006. Slow Food aims to "protect the pleasures of the table from the homogenisation of fast food and life," promotes gastronomic culture, taste education and agricultural bio-diversity, protects at-risk foods and runs university courses. It has its own publishing company which publishes books and the journal *Slow*. As Petrini put it, referring to their publications on taste education in schools, "Our books are born of sensory experiences that need to be consolidated and expressed in words" (2001: 75). Individual members meet in local groups called convivia. The movement urges individuals to integrate its principles into their everyday practices and expects convivia to promote these values through projects (for example, in schools, with local producers). The offshoot Cittàslow movement was founded in 1999. Slow Food activities are integral to Cittàslow towns. As one British Town Council found, a town will not be awarded Cittàslow status unless it has an active Slow Food convivium. Indeed, the movement states that "To achieve the status of 'Slow City', a city must agree to accept the guidelines of Slow Food and work to improve conviviality and conserve the local environment." Cittàslow treats urban contexts as spaces where slow living principles might be achieved and only town councils (or their equivalent) of towns with populations under 50,000 are eligible for

Cittàslow membership (www.cittaslow.net, www.cittaslow.org.uk) – in the UK these are usually market towns. To be accredited with Cittàslow status a UK town must fulfill fifty percent of the Cittàslow membership criteria (outlined above) and continue to develop in accordance with Cittàslow objectives.

In terms of sheer quantity of publications and other information available Slow Food undoubtedly surpasses Cittàslow. This is unsurprising since Slow Food was founded fourteen years before Cittàslow. Moreover, Cittàslow incorporates the principles of Slow Food, or, put another way, slow cities are administrative locales that extend Slow Food principles beyond just food-related practices, activities and events. As such the Slow Food manifesto and key texts such as Carlo Petrini's (2001) *Slow Food: The Case for Taste* inform not just Slow Food but also Cittàslow. It is in this spirit that I analyze them here.

Slow Living as a Sensory Project

In *The Case for Taste* Carlo Petrini proposes that social change might be achieved through reforming food practices. He laments how

> We now prefer to buy individual portions of prepackaged, presliced, and often precooked food, and opportunities to feel it, smell it, evaluate it, and compare it – in other words to know what it is we are choosing and why – are growing ever more rare (2001: 67).

Slow Food's objective to train the senses forms part of a non-militant form of resistance to this supermarket and fast-living culture, and to fast food as embodied by global hamburger chains. In Petrini's words: "Slow Food endorses the primacy of sensory experience and treats eyesight, hearing, smell, touch, and taste as so many instruments of discernment, self-defense and pleasure. The education of taste is the Slow way to resist McDonaldization" (2001: 69). As Wendy Parkins has pointed out in her analysis of how time in everyday life is reconceptualized in the discourses of the movement's publications, slow living is not intended to be a slowed down version of "fast" post-modern living. Rather, "it involves the conscious negotiation of the different temporalities which make up our everyday lives, deriving from a commitment to occupy time more attentively"and "mindfully" (Parkins 2004: 364). In Slow Food and Cittàslow literature, fundamental to this form of mindfulness is a particular type of appreciation of the sensory qualities of everyday life and the environment. Slow Food's emphasis on attentiveness and mindfulness involves a "remaking" of the everyday that "seeks to restore pleasure, agency and history to everyday life," through "an aesthetic which imbricates the material, sensual, the intellectual and the political" which is embodied in the idea of "Slow Food's pleasure principle" (Parkins 2004: 379 quoting Capatti). This is about much more than just food and indirect activism, because taste and food are so central to history, memory and locality (Petrini 2001: 76) they are also embedded in the Cittàslow principles.

In practice this means that by making sensory experience and knowledge central to Slow Food practices, they also become inseparable from the projects of conviviality, community, locality and economy that characterize Cittàslow activities. In Aylsham, Slow Food marks most Cittàslow events or processes in some way. Likewise, in locally produced Slow Food literature taste, locality and economy become inextricably interwoven. For example, at my first meeting with Sue Flack, the Partnership Officer and a central figure in Slow Food and Cittàslow in Aylsham, she gave me a copy of a short piece entitled "Where does all our money go?" about a day in the life of a five pound note that she had written for a local publication. In the story the money "was quickly handed over to the butcher to pay for a couple of nice (locally reared beef) steaks for supper," the gist of the story being that if we spend our money locally, on local produce rather than in the chain stores in bigger cities, the chances are that it will stay in and support the local economy. Sensory experience is thus central to the interrelated aesthetic and activist projects of slow living as they are presented in the rhetoric of Slow Food essay and manifesto texts.[3] Texts that refer specifically to Cittàslow are generally much shorter, more concise and are published on-line (www.cittaslow.net). Sensory experience is expressed most directly in this literature in the Cittàslow criteria document. Here there is an emphasis on urban environment and material culture with, for instance, requirements for "plans to plant sweet smelling or environment-enhancing plants in public and private gardens," "plans for the elimination of aesthetically displeasing advertisements" and "apparatus to measure noise pollution and plans to reduce it." Along with requiring a "commitment to develop a Slow Food convivium," and all its gustatory implications, the Cittàslow UK criteria document itself begins to introduce a sensory vocabulary into town planning.

Above I noted how Knox (2005) had equated Cittàslow with an urban process that inspires the sort of social construction of place that might be seen as "successful" in terms of contemporary design standards and how Malnar and Vodvarka (2004) and Pallasmaa (2005) have called for designers to disregard their occularcentric perspectives and reconceptualize the city as a multisensory space. They document recent arguments for attention to haptic, olfactory and sonic elements of urban (and spatial) experience, stressing the interrelatedness of these with visual experience (see, for example, Malnar and Vodvarka 2004: 129–52). However, Cittàslow goes beyond ideologies and urban design; it also involves emplaced individuals (Howes 2005, Feld 2005) and the constitution of place though their subjective sensory practices, experiences and projects. Cittàslow can be seen as an urban process (or set of processes) that advocates the engagement of the senses (and intersubjectivity) in the social construction of place and in urban design. Politically this calls for the creation of alternative urban "sensescapes" that implicitly critique the visual, olfactory, gustatory, sonic and haptic experiences that are associated with global consumer capitalism. However, it also acknowledges hard science in its rendering of a context for slow living. Before continuing to discuss my Cittàslow ethnography I reflect on how both scientific (objective) and experiential (subjective) notions of the sensory city are combined in Cittàslow.

The idea that existing methods of measuring urban pollution are insufficient is becoming increasingly popular in urban studies. For example, Manon Raimbault and Danièle Dubois criticize urban noise-level measurements as too limited since "Human perception of noise, in contrast to a physical instrument such as a sound level meter, is not absolute and mainly relies on the meaning of sounds." Using the concept of "soundscape" they propose an interdisciplinary approach that accounts for human subjectivity, seeing "urban soundscapes as complex sonic environments and as cues about socio-cultural life throughout history" and moreover "always perceived within a simultaneous multi-sensorial setting, in which the diverse sense modalities interact with auditory judgments" (Raimbault and Dubois 2005). Cittàslow sets out to engage with the sensory potentials of urban *space* in order to create an experienced reality of a particular kind of *place* in which are embedded certain ideals related to notions of locality, transmission of (what Petrini [2001: 70] would call "real") knowledge and the "mindfulness" (cf. Parkins 2004) noted above. Embedded within this model is, however, a tension between bureaucratic/institutionalized scientific tendencies to quantify sensory elements of urban contexts in attempts to measure "environmental quality" and phenomenological approaches to sensory experience more common in social sciences and humanities approaches. They are co-implicated because, although the quality of an urban environment might be measurable using technologies that objectify it by producing statistical evidence of air pollution, sound levels and so forth, it is simultaneously objectified when people use sensory metaphors to verbalize, enact, write about or visualize their embodied experiences of urban environments. The Cittàslow/Slow Food literature encompasses both these approaches, which may broadly be characterized as on the one hand "objective (scientific)" and on the other "(inter)subjective" ways of representing the sensory nature of urban space. While the Slow Food and Cittàslow literature emphasize sentiments that escape measurement, such as "pleasure" and "enjoyment," the Cittàslow criteria necessarily require measurement, and evaluation is needed before a town can become Cittàslow accredited. In the words of Cittàslow UK:

> The process is not arduous, and involves completing a fairly detailed questionnaire that forms a self-assessment of your town's current position. This scores your town against the Cittaslow Goals.

Most towns will be well on the way to scoring 50 percent against the Cittaslow Goals, which is a requirement of membership. Cittaslow UK can help you get to grips with Goals and how to score your town against them, and will conduct a short, formal audit of your self-assessement when you apply to join the network. (http://www.cittaslow.org.uk/)

Aylsham
Aylsham is a market town in Norfolk with a population of about 6,000 situated between the North Norfolk coastal zone, which is a popular area for wealthy incomers from London, and the region's capital city, Norwich. Aylsham has a well-kept historic picture-postcard market square and town center, and the local people I spoke to stressed a strong sense of community that they believe it would be hard to find elsewhere. Those who had led the Cittàslow application process (Liz Jones [Chair of the Cittàslow Committee and a Town Councillor], Mo Reynolds [the Town Clerk] and Sue Flack [the Aylsham Partnership Officer]) emphaisized to me that Aylsham had been accredited because it was really already doing most of the things that Cittàslow required. Jenny Manser, vice-chair of a local charity, was well-placed through the local knowledge her position afforded her, and her professional expertise, to comment that "There are places that do need regeneration and Aylsham is not one of them. What it needs, if anything, is support in order to sustain the life that we have here." However, despite being set in affluent North Norfolk, in Aylsham unemployment and rural social deprivation are recognized problems in its housing estates and in the hinterland of the town. Some Cittàslow projects contribute to addressing these issues.

In Aylsham, Slow Food and Cittàslow have been put into practice through a series of projects that create social interventions that work towards social inclusion. For example, teenagers studying catering at the high school are involved in Slow Food catering projects, a series of community garden projects of different scales are being developed and intergenerational learning projects connect ageing and youth populations. Other projects engage local people in the production of locality-based memory banks, such as a digital community archive and heritage center. The Cittàslow launch event in 2004 was a "big breakfast" in the town hall of locally produced sausages, bacon, eggs and vegetables designed in terms of its accessible price and broad appeal to be inclusive rather than to represent "foodie" culture; this event is now repeated annually, serving 150 people in two sittings. Following this narrative of local activity my fieldwork in Aylsham (on-going since 2005) follows how these and other projects are developed, experienced and participate in processes of change at three levels: local government and town council committees; local institutions, groups and organizations (for instance, local schools, societies and NGOs) and through individual practices and understandings. In this article I take an on-going Cittàslow process as a case study: the Green Lanes Community Garden Project which is converting a disused site of land in a housing area into a community garden.

The Green Lanes Community Garden Project: From Wasted Space to a Local Place

The Green Lanes Community Garden Project is concerned with the transformation of a site of land situated between the streets of a housing estate about five minutes walk from Aylsham's town center. The land is owned by the town council and was formerly a playground area but was repeatedly vandalized and had become disused. The site is almost rectangular and about seventy meters long.

The Green Lanes Community Garden project demonstrates how Cittàslow is embedded within the town at various levels. The project is implicated on the agendas of three committees: Cittàslow, the Community Gardens Steering Group (CGSG) and Green Lanes. While it certainly falls under the Cittàslow umbrella it is largely driven by Aylsham Care Trust (ACT). The CGSG is composed of members of key agencies and institutions – the Cittàslow committee, Slow Food, the Aylsham Partnership, ACT, the church and others. The Green Lanes project is its first and most developed project. The project itself with the support of the CGSG and ACT is run and developed on a day to day basis by its own committee composed of a group of neighbours directly concerned with the transformation of the land, and led by David Gibson the Chairperson. As such, while the project is not directly managed by Cittàslow, it is precisely the sort of local practical engagement with both the physical urban environment and the bureaucracies that contributes to the Cittàslow profile and identity of the town. Such projects are as much a part of Cittàslow as those (like carnival) that are directly produced by Cittàslow subcommittees. My research involves all these different levels. I attend committee meetings, interview key participants from all levels of the projects and make accompanied visits to the garden itself as it develops.

The garden site can be understood theoretically in terms of what Margaret Rodman calls "multilocality" (2003: 210–11). Multilocality implies (among other things) "seeking to understand the construction of place from multiple viewpoints" and recognizing that "a single physical landscape can be multilocal in the sense that it shapes and expresses polysemic meanings of place for different users" (2003: 12). As the example below demonstrates, individuals may also *represent* and communicate their own constructions of place in multiple ways, that is, by using photographs or maps, through walking, through being there, and through speech. The sensory nature of the garden project is conspicuous at all levels at which it is "owned," with explicit attention to its sonic, olfactory and visual elements. It was first introduced to me by Sue (Aylsham Partnership Officer) as "a rest space, a quiet space in the middle of one of the housing estates." When I asked Mo (the town clerk) to elaborate she told me that the local residents "would like a decent path through [the garden site] which would be wide enough for pushchairs and wheel chairs and a couple of benches, just somewhere to sit, and some shrubs" the plants would include, she said, "perhaps, you know, a bit of sensory stuff or whatever for people who are visually impaired or whatever." Mo stressed that it would not be "a municipal park where the flowers are in rigid lines or anything like that" but "a nice bit of open space where they can perhaps just sit and chat or whatever, and stop on the way back from shopping because as you get older you can't always chase around so much." Sue's and Mo's comments both hold echoes of the Cittàslow literature and criteria analyzed above, and indeed they were both leading figures in the town's application for Cittàslow accreditation. However, Jenny (ACT and CGSG), whose involvement with Cittàslow is much less direct, similarly told me "so they are going to have a kind of sensory bit, part of it, and also a bit that is back to nature and also a bit of raised beds so the elderly can access them a bit better." When I interviewed David (Chair of the Green Lanes committee), one of the residents who is involved "on the ground" with coordinating the design and planning process, I asked him and his wife Anne about the sensory plans for the garden. They told me there would be a section with scented flowers and herbs, showing me how this was visualized in the garden plan:

David: Highly scented
Anne: Highly scented lavenders.
David: Lavenders, herbs.
Anne: Herbs and...
David: Things like that, and shrubs that mainly attract the birds.
Anne: Butterflies.
David: Bees, butterflies and things like that, that's, I think I actually wrote in there...
Sarah: Oh yes, [reading from David's garden design plan shown in figure 1] "bees, butterflies, fragrant..."

However, once I began to research the sensory dimension of the planning as the residents themselves developed it I found it did not only refer to scented plants. I demonstrate this by focusing on the path, which was a key element of concern for all parties due to the role it would play in the garden and to its being the most costly element of the project.

Malnar and Vodvarka see paths as "generative elements of spatial design" (2004: 118). They note how although "transition through a structured space is surely familiar to all human beings ... yet the

Figure 1
David's design plan for the garden detailed the route the pathway should take, the types, colors and smells of the flowers and the materials that should be used. Photograph © Sarah Pink 2005.

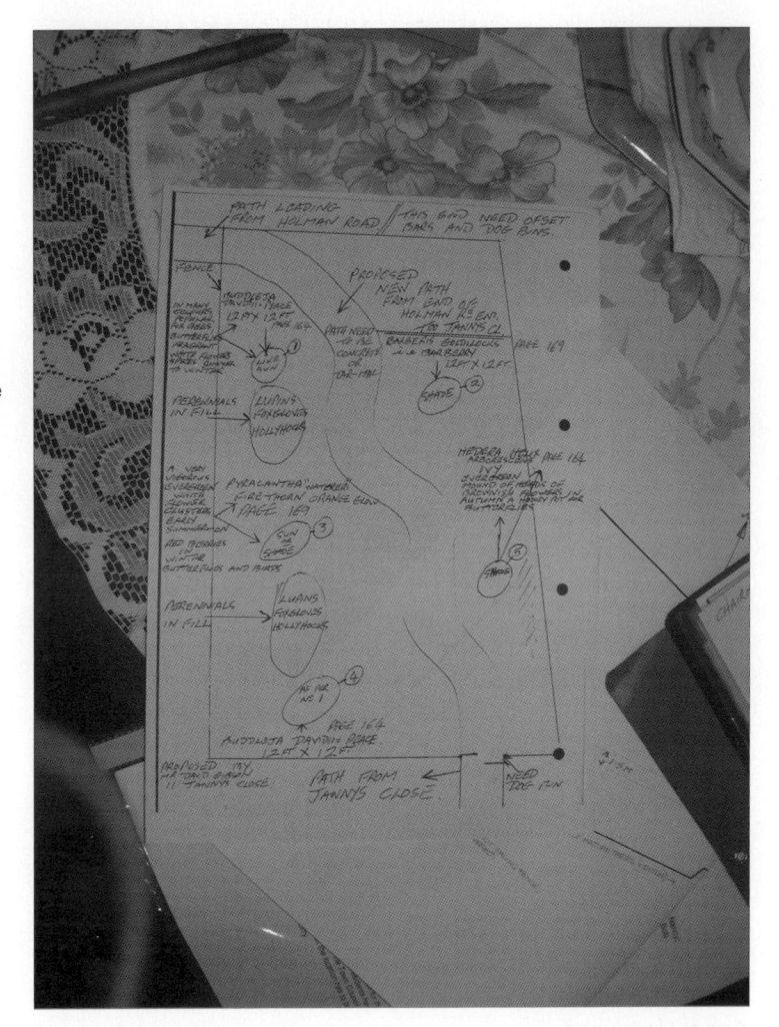

generative role of the path, and its sensory character, has seldom been given much consideration by architectural theorists" (2004: 119). Our use of pathways is intensely personal as by walking them in specific ways we appropriate urban space, as such constituting (multilocal) places though our movement (de Certeau 1984, Gray 2003) and thus through our emplaced sensory practice. Paths are clearly not simply functional routes that connect one place to another, but meaningful sensory and imaginative places their own right that interact with and are contextualized by the urban sensescapes of which they form a part. In the case of the Green Lanes project the pathway itself was a central concern; in fact, on one level, the whole project can be seen as one of creating a "pathway" as it aimed to create not only a garden but a place through which passage was possible. Here I focus on the pathway as a means of analytical

Figure 2
David, Anne and I decided that in their portrait for my research they should be holding photographs of the possible style, materials and quality of workmanship proposed for the pathway. Photograph © Sarah Pink 2005.

access to the garden for three reasons. First, it will be the route of physical access to the garden for those who use it. Second it offers a way of understanding how a particular material element of the garden is contextualized by other tangible and non-tangible elements. In the summary of suggested design ideas from one of the group's early meetings it was proposed that the path should be a "Simple path – smooth and wide." This would be contextualized by other textures and materials – shrubs and flowers, meadow/tall grass, raised flower beds, natural materials (wood), access bars (see also Figure 1). At these early stages of planning and visualization the residents were attending to the production of the sensescape of the garden. One of the problems associated with the site before development was its status as a short cut and what this meant for both the way it was experienced and how it was used. David told me that "all the mums take their children to school and they walk across here. Of course when it's wet, when it's sort of like this they tend to walk all the way round." We walked around the site ourselves in the pouring rain. Drawing from his own emplaced knowledge about the site and taking the weather as context, David advised that we stayed under the protection of the trees for as long as possible to prevent us from getting too wet and avoided the mud he pointed out underfoot. The project sought to create a dry ("smooth and wide") route across the field that would modify people's corporeal experience of the crossing as well as leading them to perceive it as an all-weathers route to town. It also, however, intended to limit the sorts of physical experiences of the route that might be had. Bars were being added at both entrances to the site to prevent cyclists from "racing through." The path would also be a route to the facilities within the garden, possibly a small grassy slope for children to slide down. Selecting the materials and textures of the new path was complex, involving economic, aesthetic, quality and time-keeping considerations. Some members of the group had gone so far as to travel to the next village to view the work of one contractor they had considered for the work, to decide that the concrete covered in stone surface he suggested was not right for their path. Instead, after considering several quotes they eventually agreed on the brickweave surface shown in Figures 3 and 4.

The importance of the role of the local residents in leading this project (as opposed to it simply being a token consultation process) is that they were well (em)placed to base their decisions on their own experiences of already having "been there." When we visited the site, David asked me if I had been able to imagine its size and scale. I had by this time seen various maps and plans and had spoken about the site with him, but, I had to reply, I had been unable to imagine it as I now experienced it. Being there was crucial and could not be replaced by having seen the maps. Up to a point my experiences would seem to coincide with Pallasmaa's view that "tactile sensibility replaces distancing visual imagery though enhanced materiality, nearness and intimacy" (2005: 323). However, to understand any visual image, including maps, we need to situate them in relation to the contexts of their production and interpretation rather than simply analyze their visual content (Pink 2001, Banks 2001). In this fieldwork experience, the supposed dominance of objectifying visual mapping over sensuous subjectivity did not underlie David's treatment of the task of "showing" me the site: there was no question of "being there" being unnecessary even though it was pouring with rain.[4] Following Tim Ingold (2000), and as I have earlier implied in my own research about "the sensory home" (Pink 2004), I suggest it is not so much a matter of modern Western culture being utterly permeated by the dominance of objectifying and distancing visual ways of understanding, rather it is up to the ethnographer to refocus on how people actually *do* inhabit, recognize and purposefully create multisensory environments. In everyday life it seems to me that objectifying visualizations and emplaced haptic, sonic, olfactory and gustatory experiences work in combination. If visualizations objectify then the question should be one of *what* does the map objectify. Visual meanings are always contextual. When situated in relation to the sensory meanings, emplaced knowledge and local intersubjectivity that informed the production of David's map there is nothing alienating about it. Rather, when an academic analysis of it is rooted in an understanding of what it actually refers to and communicates about, it might be understood as an evocative text that conveys sensory experience, knowledge and creative imaginings.

Returning to Cittàslow as an umbrella project for the Green Lanes Community Garden, the greater significance of Cittàslow as a sensory approach to urban planning and design becomes evident. Framed

Sensing Cittàslow: Slow Living and the Constitution of the Sensory City

Figure 3
In mid March 2006 Monica, the administrator supporting the CGSG and Green Lanes committees emailed me this photograph of the newly completed path. Photograph © David Gibson 2005.

Figure 4
The path in summer 2006 once planting was underway. Photograph © Sarah Pink 2005.

by Cittàslow the project directly represents some of its criteria, for example: "[the] existence of well kept green spaces"; "places for people to sit down and rest, not just in town centres" and "plans to plant sweet smelling or environment-enhancing plants in public or private gardens." By using local residents' emplaced knowledge to inform the planning and design of the garden this Cittàslow project is able to incorporate the intersubjective and experiential dimension of urban life into a planning process that otherwise relies on visualizations and planning permissions, insurance and risk assessment. As such the project can be seen as a sensory intervention, a form of sensory creativity that creates a meaningful multilocality within the urban context.

A Comparative Reflection: Cittàslow Carnival

In the previous section I focused on one type of Cittàslow practice – a project. Although there is no space here to develop further detailed case studies of others,[5] it is worth briefly pointing out some parallels.

In the summer of 2005 Aylsham revived its lapsed carnival as part of its Cittàslow calendar of events. There are many ways this carnival might be analyzed, not least in relation to the wider literature on carnival contestation and protest.[6] However, here I focus on the process by which Carnival is produced through sensory-spatial design. I have attended carnival committee meetings and the carnival itself as a participant observer and interviewed participants. The carnival is an event that unites multiple agencies across the town to take responsibility for and contribute their expert knowledge to different aspects of the event. During the planning meetings I attended I was struck by how the discussions of the spatial organization of the carnival were never accompanied by a map of the town. For example, committee members spoke about where music would be spaced around the town (a band, an accordion player, steel drums etc...) using their own emplaced experiential knowledge of being in the town to subjectively imagine how these different sonic positionings would create a certain urban soundscape. Likewise, an urban carnival tastescape was created: in the town hall teenagers fundraising for their own Slow Food Trip to an Italian food festival sold cakes and tea they had made, outside was parked a van selling locally made ice cream from nearby Great Yarmouth and up the street were the local Quakers giving away their flapjacks. Carnival in Alysham is a planning process and an event that engages emplaced experience, knowledge and practice to creatively produce a specific multisensory context though practices that objectify Cittàslow and Slow Food ideologies and moralities. Carnival conspicuously appropriates local space to "turn up-side down" the "outside" (global) world of consumer capitalism, for instance by closing itself to ice cream and burger vans representing global business and instead inviting people to taste ice cream and meat produced locally (see

Pink 2006). It is a good example of how Cittàslow "provides a site where agency can be exercised in the face of the 'inevitabilities' of global culture" (Parkins and Craig 2006: 83).

Above I noted how the objective (scientific) and (inter)subjective (experiential) elements of the sensory city combine and are interdependent in Cittàslow. These principles are also evident in carnival planning. Procedures for risk assessment in the UK and health and safety regulations must be respected while the sorts of sensory experiences available are indicated by Cittàslow and Slow Food though an emphasis on the local. Local people have subjective, experiential knowledge of the town generated by their emplaced habitation and navigation of its buildings and streets in their everyday lives. This local form of knowing is verbalized in committee discussions about where best to hear the band, see visual displays and taste local foods, and it informs the production of the carnival as a multisensory urban event. Therefore, like the community garden project, the production of the Cittàslow carnival is a sensory intervention. Within a circumscribed period of time it creates an alternative sensescape to that constituted through the agencies of global capitalism.

Final Thoughts

Any city and the events and projects that form part of the everyday and festive practices that create locality and place within it could be analyzed as multisensory. However, in a Cittàslow town these elements of knowledge, experience, practice and creativity come to the fore in very particular ways. The sensory nature of pleasure and calls for a reeducation of the senses abound in the Slow Food and Cittàslow literature. Moreover the sorts of intersubjectivity and local participation that Knox (2005) suggests underlie the success of Cittàslow as a form of urban planning seem to encourage an approach to the mutual constitution of the city and self that draws from individuals' emplaced sensory experience.

Notes

1. For example, in a way that echoes Petrini's (2001) calls for sensory (re)education, as discussed below, Pallasmaa proposes that "the education of the sense and of the imagination is necessary for a full and dignified life" (2005: 140).
2. Generously funded by Loughborough University (2005–6) and by the Nuffield Foundation (2006–7).
3. Here I use the term "aesthetic" in the sense that Bull et al. suggest when they propose a return to the "original meaning of the term 'aesthetic' not as a form of judgment but as the *disposition to sense acutely*" (2006: 6)
4. As James Fernandez has pointed out, this is characteristic of an anthropological approach in which the researcher makes "an

effort to turn the spaces we go out to inhabit into places with whose feeling tones we are familiar" (2003: 187).
5. These will be the topics of future papers
6. For example, because Cittàslow carnival is already underwritten with an activist protest stance that is owned by the power holders. However I do not deal with this here.

References

Amin, A. and Thrift, N. 2002. *Cities: Reimagining the Urban*. Cambridge: Polity Press.

Banks, M. 2001. *Visual Methods in Social Research*. London: Sage.

Bull, M., Gilroy, P., Howes, D. and Kahn, D. 2006. Introduction to *Senses and Society*, 1(1): 5–7.

De Certeau, M. 1984. *The Practice of Everyday Life*. London: University of California Press.

Desjarlais, R. 2003. *Sensory Biographies: Lives and Death among Nepal's Yolmo Buddhists*. London: University of California Press.

———. 2005. "Movement, Stillness: On the Sensory World of a Shelter for the Homeless Mentally Ill." In David Howes (ed.), *Empire of the Senses: The Sensory Culture Reader*. Oxford: Berg.

Feld, S. 2005. "Places Sensed, Senses Placed: Towards a Sensuous Epistemology of Environments." In David Howes (ed.), *Empire of the Senses: The Sensory Culture Reader*. Oxford: Berg.

Fernandez, J. 2003. "Emergence and Convergence in some African Sacred Places." In Setha M. Low and Denise Lawrence-Zuniga (eds), *The Anthropology of Space and Place: Locating Culture*. Oxford: Blackwell.

Geurts, K. L. 2002. *Culture and the Senses: Bodily Ways of Knowing in an African Community*. Berkeley, Los Angeles, London: University of California Press.

Gray, J. (2003) "Open Spaces and Dwelling Places: Being at Home on Hill Farms in the Scottish Borders' Places." In Setha M. Low and Denise Lawrence-Zuniga (eds), *The Anthropology of Space and Place: Locating Culture*. Oxford: Blackwell.

Howes, D. 2005. "Introduction." In David Howes (ed.), *Empire of the Senses: The Sensory Culture Reader*. Oxford: Berg.

Ingold, T. 2000. *The Perception of the Environment*. London: Routledge.

Knox, P. 2005. "Creating Ordinary Places: Slow Cities in a Fast World." *Journal of Urban Design*, 10(1): 1–11.

Law, L. 2005. "Home Cooking: Filipino Women and Geographies of the Senses in Hong Kong." In David Howes (ed.), *Empire of the Senses: The Sensory Culture Reader*. Oxford: Berg.

Malnar, J. and Vodvarka , F. 2004. *Sensory Design*. Minneapolis, MI: University of Minnesota Press.

Miller, D. 2001. "Behind Closed Doors." In D. Miller (ed.) *Home Possessions*. Oxford: Berg.

Pallasmaa, J. [1999] 2005. "Lived Space: Embodied Experience and Sensory Thought." In *Encounters: Architectural Essays*. Hämeenlinna, Finland: Rakennustieto Oy.

Parkins, W. 2004. "Out of Time: Fast Subjects and Slow Living." In *Time and Society*, 13(2–3): 363–82.

Parkins, W. and Craig, G. 2006. *Slow Living*. Oxford: Berg.

Petrini, C. 2001. *Slow Food: The Case for Taste*. New York: Columbia University Press.

Pink, S. 2001. *Doing Visual Ethnography*. London: Sage.

——. 2004. *Home Truths*. Oxford: Berg.

——. 2006. "Slow Cosmopolitans." Paper presented at the ASA conference, Keele.

Raimbault, M. and Dubois, D. 2005. "Urban Soundscapes: Experiences and Knowledge."*Cities*, 22 (5): 339–50.

Rodman, M. 2003. "Empowering Place: Multivocality and Multi-locality." In S.M. Low and D. Lawrence-Zuniga (eds), *The Anthropology of Space and Place: Locating Culture*. Oxford: Blackwell.

Stewart, P. and Strathern, A. 2003. "Introduction." In P. Stewart and A. Strathern (eds), *Landscape, Memory and History*. London: Pluto Press.

The Slow Food Companion (2005). Available online: http://www.slowfood.com/eng/sf_cose/sf_cose_companion.lasso (accessed September 18, 2006).

Turner, V. 1986. "Dewey, Dilthey and Drama: An Essay in the Anthropology of Experience." In V. Turner and E. Brunner (eds), *The Anthropology of Experience*. Urbana, IL: University of Illinois Press.

THE ANIMALS READER
The Essential Classic and Contemporary Writings

Edited by Linda Kalof and Amy Fitzgerald

"...from Aristotle to postmodern philosophers...

...from orangutans to cyborgs...

The Animals Reader presents a wonderful diversity of perspectives on animals and, in consequence, ourselves."

Boria Sax, author of *Crow, Animals in the Third Reich* and *The Mythical Zoo*

The study of animals – and the relationship between humans and other animals – is now one of the most fiercely debated topics in contemporary science and culture. As the first book of its kind, *The Animals Reader* provides a framework for understanding the current state of the multidisciplinary field of animal studies. This anthology will be invaluable for students across the Humanities and Social Sciences as well as for general readers.

Contributors Include:

Aristotle • Steve Baker • Marc Bekoff • Jeremy Bentham • John Berger • Jonathan Burt
Gilles Deleuze • Descartes • Donna Haraway • Lévi-Strauss • Randy Malamud • Steven Mithen
Michel de Montaigne • Martha Nussbaum • Pliny • Plutarch • Tom Regan • Harriet Ritvo
Boria Sax • Peter Singer • Marjorie Spiegel • Yi-Fu Tuan • Sarah Whatmore

February 2007 • 448pp • 10 b/w illus
ISBN 978 1 84520 470 9 (PB) £19.99 • $34.95
ISBN 978 1 84520 469 3 (HB) £60.00 • $105.00
www.bergpublishers.com

BERG

Sensory Design

Les Cols Restaurant: A Sensual Feast

Elias Vavaroutsos

Elias Vavaroutsos is a lead designer with OWP/P Architects in Chicago and a visiting studio critic at the University of Illinois at Urbana-Champaign.
evavaroutsos@owpp.com

Like the sensual cuisine and landscape from which it draws meaning and associative content, the architecture of Les Cols Restaurant is a virtual study in sensory dynamism muted by an overall mood of repose. Established in 1990, Les Cols ("the cauliflowers") is the passion of chef and owner Fina Puigdevall, who looks to nature for inspiration in creating offerings of "intimacy and sensory pleasure" rooted to the surrounding landscape.[1] The restaurant is located at the fringes of Olot, a remote town in the volcanic La Garrotxa region of northern Spain near the southern foothills of the Pyrenees, seventy-five kilometers inland from the Mediterranean Sea.

The power of nature is felt on a daily basis around Olot. Its distinct character is determined by expansive views of mountains and valleys, primordial landforms of diverse color and texture, volcanic cones, perched settlements and monumental layers of basalt strata. The River Fluvia winds across this humid region and through Olot, at times cooling the air and bringing forth evanescent mists that envelop the landscape in a dreamlike and floating ambience. In the pervasive sensation of moisture on the skin, the fleeting aromas of oak wood and beech forests and the haptic terrain of ejected volcanic material underfoot, the natural phenomena around Olot provide endless opportunities for "potential transactions between body, imagination, and environment" (Moore and Bloomer 1977: 105).

In 2001, Ms Puigdevall asked local architects RCR-Aranda Pigem Vilalta to transform the former ground floor stables of the sixteenth-century stone farmhouse where she was born into an inviting setting suited to Les Cols's emerging presence as a culinary experience of international acclaim. RCR's sensibility has been profoundly influenced by the potent landscape surrounding Olot. Their intent is to concentrate and intensify simultaneously the sensual perception of the natural world's primitive aura and the awareness of the silence of the self by means of relying upon empathy to communicate directly with the senses, emotions and imagination. At Les Cols, RCR explores the sensory capacities of steel with the intent to "enhance the joy of life by appealing to the senses" (Curtis 2004: 43).

The new structure is a 6,500 square-foot one-story insertion of glass and steel into the vaulted ground-floor space of the original stone farm, linking the two semicircular gardens at each end. The restaurant is approached indirectly through a pre-existing brick portico leading into the first garden. With its tall hedges and embracing form, the garden has a protective quality. The spatial experience is intensified by the aroma of fruit trees in bloom and an abrupt insular silence broken only by the sound of the visitor's own footfalls and the clucking of the garden's free-range chickens. From the garden, the visitor may perceive the restaurant as a long, low volume of transparent, frameless glass behind a veil of intertwined steel ribbons vaguely reminiscent of vegetation (perhaps an abstraction of the climbing vines so germane to the owner's childhood experience).

Rusted steel planks laid in the grass guide the route to the entry. Upraised dents in their surface (not unlike bosses of Inca stonework) add visual tactility and relief to the otherwise smooth surface. While this detail intrigues the eye it more importantly reveals the architect's empathic directness in detailing; the raised dents caress the soles of the visitor's feet and encourage a slow gait while providing practical footing, considering the frequent rains. One might even imagine visitors traversing the route, then unexpectedly delighted, walking backwards and retracing their steps. The two planks in the grass act as steps, carefully guiding the feet up onto a small platform in front of the entrance door.

At the end of the planks, the axis of approach shifts. The visitor is drawn to the right by means of the platform's shadowy recess. Here, an inviting pool of water slips beneath a metal trellis suspending a secretive cloak of ivy. The semipermeable veil permits glimpses of activity in the kitchen beyond; the visitor might perceive the silhouettes of chefs in motion, or their reflections upon the pool of water. Along with the aroma of the ivy, this almost cinematic foreshadowing heightens the anticipation of a memorable culinary experience and offers the opacity, depth and mystery so alluring

Figure 1
Pathway, Les Cols
Restaurant. Photograph
© Elias Vavaroutsos, 2006.

to the senses. In its indirect and unhurried approach, Les Cols's entry sequence recalls the stone paths, shifting axes and non-linear movements through thresholds of deep shadow characteristic of Zen garden and temple complexes. This is not surprising, given RCR's familiarity with and affinity for traditional Japanese architecture and the gardens of Kyoto.

Seemingly composed of narrow stone paving, the floor of the entry platform is actually of natural steel and continues inside through a pivoting glass door. Yet this portal is transparent to the gaze and bodily engaging, silently swinging open with the barest touch. Upon entering the restaurant, the visitor encounters the main dining area ahead and a reception zone to the right. The dining room is arranged in small seating groups along a wall of frameless glass at eye level with an elevated portion of garden (and its chickens) beyond. Dark, oxidized steel walls and screens of twisted steel ribbons perpendicular to the glass suggest intimate boundaries for the seating groups and lend an earthy atmosphere to the room.

The dining room's steel tables and chairs by RCR are cut and folded like abstracted floral origami, and finished in lustrous gold enamel. Despite their visual delicacy, the visitor might expect to find the chairs hard and unyielding. An unconscious element of touch is concealed in the sense of vision; as we observe, so the eye feels the hardness, texture, temperature and weight of the surfaces (Pallasmaa 2006: 143). In fact, the chairs' curving back and single arm encourage a slight recline and a posture of ease and relaxation. One senses a tension in the stark contrast of their fluid smoothness with the textured vault ceilings and walls of the original structure. The brilliant reflective glow of these objects is set off against the subdued hues of purple, blue and brown on the raw steel floor.

Despite its variegated appearance and visual similarity to wood, the floor has none of the feel or liveliness of wood; following the wonderful experience of the upraised dents of steel outside, the visitor might have enjoyed the continued experience of Le Cols quite literally, *by foot*.

To the right of the entry, two tall, rectilinear steel objects without obvious means of access mark the reception area. These mute volumes function as serving drawers for wines, glasses and menus; like simplified Japanese puzzle boxes they willingly slide open with the gentlest pressure of the hand ... yielding the treasures within. The motif is repeated in the nearby restrooms where cool, sleek partitions float in a vaulted space seemingly without support or means of access, swinging open silently by means of the body's encounter.

Adjacent to the reception area, secretive vertical openings reveal the inner workings of the kitchen; a functional space of measured exactness sheathed in stainless steel. The kitchen is shaped around a sky-lit patio walled in frameless glass. At the base of this light-filled void, a reflecting pool extends out to the previously encountered entry platform and floating screen of ivy. The cool bluish cast and hard-edged forms contrast the warm, organic dining environment and illustrates the architects' interest in one changing perceptions as one moves around. Thus, where vision is concerned, the sensory realm of events is perceived in fragments – through a slot, beyond a filigree of luminous steel vegetation, behind a wall or beneath a surface. At Les Cols, peripheral and fragmentary perceptions transform retinal images into spatial and bodily enigma, encouraging sensory thought and participation.

Beyond the reception area is Les Col's tour-de-force, a refectory-like banquet room occupying the entire length of the farmhouse structure, and opening to the second semicircular garden. The space's emphatic linearity and tunnel-like proportion are heightened by the presence of a table sixty feet in length with seating for fifty, again rendered as golden floral objects. At the room's periphery, twisting ribbons of gold-enameled steel float over the textured masonry walls of the farmhouse, vibrating in the lustrous glow of continuous florescent lighting at the ceiling and floor. Light bouncing off the lamellate wall adds a palpable sensation of heat to the sensually provocative interior.

Like its architectural reforms, Les Cols' cuisine has a lot to say with relatively few elements and highlights the contrast of tradition and avante-garde. Its signature twelve-course meals are based upon the traditional vegetable garden and local products of La Garroxta; buckwheat potatoes, corn, country poultry (ducks, chicken), local beans, the local walnut liqueur, pork and cured sausages, trout, snails, wild boar, truffles, chestnuts, turnips, mushrooms and eucalyptus flowers. Unexpected combinations like lamb shoulder (slow cooked for eleven hours) served with a sheep's-milk custard result in flavorsome, savory textures that provide the culmination of an intimate sensory experience. Ms Puigdevall offers intimate and familiar meals reinterpreting and products of the land and her surroundings with modern Spanish techniques to create understated dishes in which only what is essential remains. Clearly, the ideas that have inspired her cuisine have also defined the architectural experience.

Les Cols Restaurant is an artificial garden highlighting the juxtaposition of the man made and the natural in order to intensify a restorative and humane dining experience. A once dark, enclosed and seemingly subterranean environment has been transformed into a masterpiece of empathic architecture; multisensorial, intimate and responsive. In Les Cols, RCR Aranda Pigem Vilalta and Fina Puigdevall have created an environment imbued with significance, which, "finding echoes in the measurements of our body … expresses our relationship with the world, but at the same time reinforces our self-identity" (Pallasmaa 2006: 76).

Note
1. For the Puigdevall quotation, interview with the chef–owner by the author. Olot, September 2004.

References
Curtis, William J.R. 2004. *Between Abstraction and Nature: The Architecture of RCR Aranda Pigem Vilalta Arquitectes*. Barcelona: Gustavo Gili, SA.

Moore, Charles and Bloomer, Kent. 1977. *Body, Memory and Architecture*. New Haven: Yale University Press.

Pallasmaa, Juhani. 2006. *Encounters: Architectural Essays*. Edited by Peter MacKeith. Helsinki: Rakennustieto Oy (Building Information Ltd).

aromatherapy
today

NOW in its

10th

year of publication

written by aromatherapists for aromatherapists and health care professionals

Why do aromatherapists read aromatherapy today?

"a wonderful combination of interesting information and a good read"

"its aromatherapy with attitude"

"keeps me up to date and offers an international perspective"

email: jennifer@aromatherapytoday.com
secure website: www.aromatherapytoday.com

Midwest Skyspace

Frank Vodvarka

Frank Vodvarka is Professor of Fine Arts, Loyola University, Chicago.
http://www.frankvodvarka.com/

Yet another of James Turrell's many Skyspaces recently opened on the urban campus of the University of Illinois Chicago. Turrell has been designing such viewing chambers for more than thirty years now, primarily – though not entirely – at Redon Crater, an extinct volcano in northern Arizona. While each of these "sensing" spaces is unique, what they have in common is the power to mesmerize an audience. It is a power based on both his unabashedly mystical vision about the nature and meaning of light and the more straightforward characteristics of visual perception.

Turrell refers to that vision when he recounts: "My grandmother used to tell me that as you sat in Quaker silence you were to go inside to greet the light" (Whittaker: n.d.). He continues:

> there is an idea, first of all, of vision fully formed with the eyes closed… And the idea that it's possible to actually work in a way, on the outside, to remind one of how we see on the inside, is something that became more interesting to me as an artist. (Whittaker: n.d.)

The more prosaic aspect of his work – the actual mechanics of figure-ground perception – is the way in which this vision becomes embodied. Here he relies on a classic design phenomenon in which figure and ground, or field, have the capacity to reverse, so that the nominally negative area becomes figural in nature. In Turrell's spaces, the overhead opening – an oculus, really – reveals a sky whose light intensity and texture are greater than the solid, half-tone area of the roof. The net effect is that the sky becomes more tangible, and much closer to the viewer than the structure. It is both oddly disconcerting and profoundly beautiful to experience.

The Roden Crater Skyspaces are, of course, isolated, and thus under Turrell's control. One suspects he prefers it that way as he clearly believes these spaces benefit from an unbroken silence. In April 2006, one of his skyspaces opened in a nineteenth-century deer shelter located in the Yorkshire Sculpture Park in England. The oculus in this instance is rectangular, and the setting one of quiet semi-isolation. Caroline Lewis refers to this aspect when she says: "The work does not affect the landscape or disturb the tranquility of the site, but harnesses the changing light of the Yorkshire sky in a peaceful chamber" (Lewis: n.d.). It is precisely this aspect – the tranquility – that is not present in the University of Illinois installation.

Located at the southern end of the sprawling university campus, the skyspace is sited on a corner where two very busy urban thoroughfares intersect. While it serves as the focal point of a medium-sized plaza, it is in fact not located towards the rear of the space but rather close to the intersection. The structure is elliptical, some forty-three feet across and twenty-six feet high. The perimeter is comprised of a continuous wall of columns with concrete benches designed to match the curve of the structure. The oculus itself is oval in nature, allowing for a clear view of the sky, which – depending on time of day and weather conditions – can be bright and/or cloud-textured, or dull and continuous. Curiously, it seems most effective during overcast days, when the oval takes on the characteristics of an even, fluorescent-light fixture. Even the light falling on the underside of the roof and surrounding the oculus has been carefully controlled to achieve a middle tonality relative to the brightness of the opening.

The evening hours provide quite a different experience. The structure's interior walls have a fairly wide, unbroken band of lighting panels that glow with a colored light that continuously changes from blue to green to violet and so forth. If the intent was to form a relationship with the oculus, it fails utterly. The colored light is so vivid as to entirely "upstage" the oculus, which during daylight hours is the point of the installation. The net effect is to make the oculus secondary, if indeed it is noticed at all. While it is true that not all the hues are equally effective – the green is particularly noxious – none of them really relate to whatever the sky view has to offer. A solution might be a simple continuation of white light, which would maintain the halftone aspect. Such lighting could be controlled by sensors measuring ambient light so as to constantly adjust it to the events

Figure 1
James Turrell's Skyspace.
Photograph © Frank
Vodvarka, 2006.

seen in the oculus. Or some such. The colored lighting is carried outside the pavilion to an adjacent fountain whose rising jets of water are colored with a similar palette. Finally, blue lights are sunk in the plaza in a pattern calculated to draw attention to the pavilion and fountain. While the total effect is entirely in keeping with the theatrical lighting approach that is current Chicago public policy, it subverts the experience that Turrell has created during daylight hours. Past sundown, the pavilion becomes, for all apparent purposes, a simple colored light show.

While the light aspects are effective – at least diurnally – other sensory attributes have taken on less expected roles as a result of the site. The interruptive effects of the not inconsiderable street noise are mitigated by curtains of water falling between the columns. The university website notes that these cascades of water contribute

Figure 2
James Turrell's Skyspace.
Photograph © Frank
Vodvarka, 2006.

"to the overall tranquil character of the skyspace" (UIC: n.d.). Well … not on the several occasions I was there. Indeed, it is really too much to hope that any amount of water could mask that volume of traffic. The effect was not necessarily a negative one however. The two sorts of sound – one a reference to majestic nature, the other an unbridled urban cacophony – played off each other in a strange sort of counterpoint, adding their decibels rather than canceling them out. The sound is oddly contemporary, lending a similar character to the oval of light. It turned out that one of the days I chose for my experience was windy, and a fine spray coated both the cold bench and its occupant. The result was a largely unintended experience involving sight, sound and certain haptic attributes, whose sum was probably quite different from any of Turrell's other skyspaces.

The great strength of Turrell's spaces is that they are open to visual interpretation and to the emotional set we bring to them. He says,

> I make spaces that apprehend light for our perception, and in some way gather it, or seem to hold it. So in that way it's a little bit like Plato's cave. We sit in the cave with our backs to reality, looking at the reflection of reality on the cave wall. As an analogy to how we perceive, and the imperfections of perception, I think this is very interesting. (Whittaker)

Thus they are receptacles in which we can experience a heightened sense of sensory being, even if that heightened sense is based on a faulty premise. If that is the case, Turrell's lack of complete control at the campus site has resulted in a multisensorial experience – based also on incomplete information – that goes beyond the visual. While purists, perhaps Turrell himself, will find that annoying, it is an experience that I found oddly satisfying and, well, profoundly urban.

References

Lewis, C. n.d. "James Turrell Skyspace Opens At Yorkshire Sculpture Park." *24 Hour Museum*. http://www.24hourmuseum.org.uk/leeds/news/ART36996.html (accessed May 22, 2006).

UIC Skyspace: James Turrell. n.d. http://www.uic.edu/aa/college/turrell/1_skyspace/skyspaceFrame.htm (accessed May 22, 2006).

Whittaker, R. n.d. "Greeting the Light: An Interview with James Turrell." *Works + Conversations*. Issue 2 http://www.conversations.org/99-1-turrell.htm (accessed May 22, 2006).

ART:
Key Contemporary Thinkers

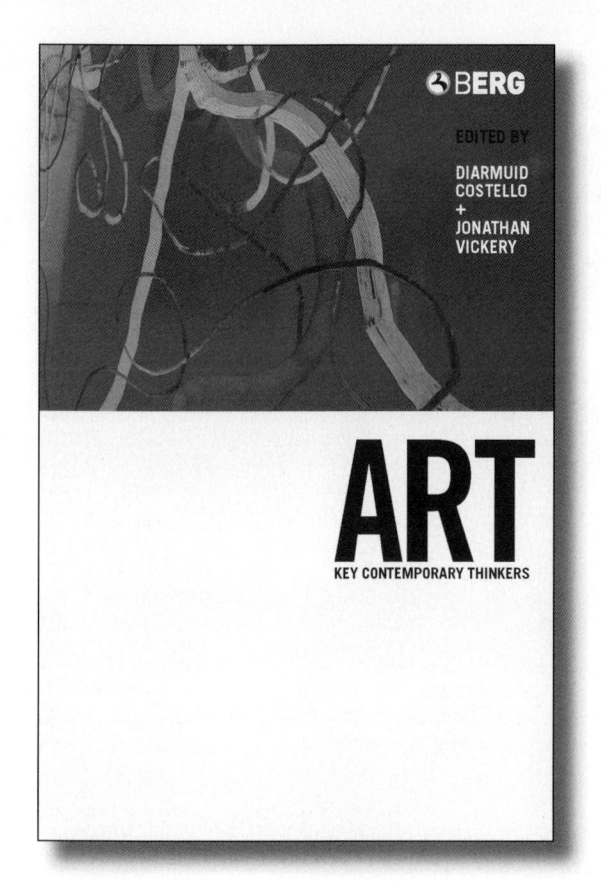

Edited by Diarmuid Costello and Jonathan Vickery

The last few decades have witnessed an explosion in ideas and theories on art. Art itself has never been more popular, but much recent thinking remains inaccessible and difficult to use. This book assesses the work of leading thinkers (including artists) who are having a major impact on making, criticizing and interpreting art. Each entry, written by a leading international expert, presents a concise, critical appraisal of a thinker and their contribution to thought about art and its place in the wider cultural context. A guide to the key thinkers who shape today's world of art, this book is a vital reference for anyone interested in modern and contemporary art, its history, theory, philosophy and practice.

- ADORNO
- BENJAMIN
- BUCHLOH
- CAVELL
- DERRIDA
- FOSTER
- GREENBERG
- KLEIN
- KRUGER
- MITCHELL
- POLLOCK
- WOLLHEIM

- BARTHES
- BERNSTEIN
- BUREN
- CLARK
- DICKIE
- FOUCAULT
- JAMESON
- KOSUTH
- LUHMANN
- MORRIS
- SMITHSON

- BATAILLE
- BOURDIEU
- BUTLER
- DANTO
- DE DUVE
- FRIED
- KELLEY
- KRAUSS
- LYOTARD
- NOCHLIN
- WALL

- BAUDRILLARD
- BOURRIAUD
- CARROLL
- DELEUZE
- ELKINS
- GRAHAM
- KELLY
- KRISTEVA
- MERLEAU-PONTY
- PIPER
- WELLMER

January 2007 • 256pp
ISBN 978 1 84520 320 7 (PB) £12.99 • $19.95
ISBN 978 1 84520 319 1 (HB) £50.00 • $94.95
www.bergpublishers.com

BERG

IIT Muffles the L: The McCormick-Tribune Campus Center

Joy Monice Malnar

Joy Monice Malnar is Associate Professor of Architecture at the University of Illinois at Urbana-Champaign.
malnar@uiuc.edu

Chicago's sonic identity is dominated by its mass transit system. With trains running on 122 miles of elevated track (locally referred to as the L) and buses on 2,273 miles of road, the sounds of their movement relentlessly fills the air. The Chicago Transit Authority proudly points out: "More than 95% of Chicago's 2.8 million population lives within a five-minute walk of regular bus or rapid transit service" (Chicago Transit Authority 1996: i). This also means that ninety-five percent of Chicago's population can, to varying degrees, hear the rumble of those trains and buses. But of the two sounds it is the elevated train, with its ability to reach 120 decibels, that is usually regarded as being responsible for the Chicago *soundscape*.

The historical approach has been to build the L tracks above the city's back alleys, using the unfortunate adjacent buildings as sound buffers. The McCormick-Tribune Campus Center, the newest building on the Illinois Institute of Technology's campus (and located next to the L) was designed by architect Rem Koolhaas, Pritzker Prize winner and principal of the Office for Metropolitan Architecture of Rotterdam. Responding to what he called an "acoustic disaster zone," Koolhaas took the unusual approach of sliding the building directly under the tracks, and then encasing the existing overhead tracks in a 530-foot "acoustic" tube. This method required 9,200 cubic yards of concrete to reduce sound conduction because the L's volume and vibration is extreme in this location. Much has been said about the eye-catching nature of the shiny, corrugated steel tube. But the photogenic tube's real purpose is to reduce the decibels of passing trains to a barely audible level inside the new building.[1] This raises a question about the actual nature of the solution: whether it is primarily a sound reduction device (as advertised) or, instead, an icon to enhance the campus' avant-garde identity.

Chicago is known not only as a railroad capital, but also as the world capital of the blues. The popular Frommer's tour guide says: "If Chicagoans were asked to pick one musical style to represent the city, most of us would start singing the blues" (Blackwell 2004: 266). And Chicago is second only to New Orleans for jazz, a result of black musicians migrating north along the rails in the 1920s. In *Soundscape*, R. Murray Schafer notes the belief of his colleague Howard Broomfield "that railroads had an important influence on the development of jazz" (Schafer 1994: 113). Broomfield

> claims blues notes (slides from major to minor thirds and sevenths) can be heard in the wail of the old steam whistles. Also, the similarity between the clickety-clack of wheels over track ends, and the drumbeats (particularly the flam, the ruff and the paradiddle) of jazz and rock music is too obvious to go unnoticed. (Schafer 1994: 113)

Schafer says he became convinced after listening to the tape mixes Broomfield made to prove his point. And the L, not to belabor the point, is very much a railroad.

The unique, droning quality of the L is created by the 55-mile-per-hour speed of the car, and the distance between the train's wheels as they pass over the joint-connections of the steel track. The acceleration and deceleration as the cars make their station stops is perceptible against the contrasting moment of silence as the passengers get on and off the train. The frequent train schedule – one train every eight minutes – is a good indicator of the pulse of the city. If Broomfield's theory that the railways were influential in the development of two major forms of music – blues and jazz – is reasonable, then one has to wonder why Chicago's architecture has not been influenced by the railroads. It is therefore regrettable that the rhythmic sound of the L at this site was only muffled, and not treated as a design element.

IIT's campus, with its master plan and twenty-two of its buildings designed by Ludwig Mies van der Rohe through the 1940s and '50s, is considered an archetype of modernism. In contrast, the south-side elevated tracks that pass through the campus are the oldest

Figure 1
The McCormick-Tribune Campus Center and the L. Photograph © Joy Monice Malnar 2006.

in the city, built in 1892 and later extended to Hyde Park to service the Colombian Exposition World's Fair of 1893. While IIT was itself founded in 1890, it was Mies's master plan that made the tracks a central element of the campus. Chicago realtors know that property value is based on a fine balance that occurs between walking convenience to the L and sonic distance from the L. The L can achieve a noise level that not only disrupts normal communication and concentration but can have a negative impact on our emotional well-being. Thus the L – and any alteration to it – has both sonic and economic dimensions.

How does the tube design fare? Unfortunately, while the train's passage is barely audible within the building – clearly a success - the sound for the train passengers is louder within the concrete tube. While designed for IIT's students and faculty, it offers little consideration for the Chicago Transit Authority's riders or for that matter the Illinois tax payers. The tube cost 13.6 million dollars, nine million coming from a grant from the state's Illinois First program. "The tube is an amazing engineering feat," said IIT President Lew Collens. "It provides an important prototype for solving acoustical problems that limit land uses near elevated tracks in many cities."[2] But at $25,660 per linear foot of tube it is ridiculous to think that it can serve as a prototype for the 122 miles of elevated track. Indeed, why should it even be considered a good solution, since it intensifies the noise within the tube and blocks the rider's view of the city.

Even more surprising, given the tube's cost, is that apparently only its exterior form matters. While it looks like a landmark train station, it is not; the train speeds through the tube without stopping. In fact, there is no way ever to experience being surrounded by it. The skylight-like, orange fins are only used as openings to allow sound to escape and so lessen some of the impact on CTA riders. Ironically, within view of the tube is S.R. Crown Hall, one of Mies's greatest creations. One can only imagine what a wonderful complement the elliptical interior space of the tube could have been to the rectangular Crown Hall.

The main part of the building – that portion under the tube – stands in sharp contrast to the tube itself, and is a positive addition to the campus. Like many areas on the south side of Chicago, this once-vital area was cleared in the 1940s in the name of urban renewal. Koolhaas was intent on mitigating the destructive aspects of this phenomenon by reestablishing the built density necessary to the urban experience. Koolhaas felt it was important to exploit the "pathways" already created by the students as they moved between dorms located on the east side of the tracks and classrooms on the west side. He and a group of students documented the direct routes that crossed the parking lot and used them to establish the building footprint. Thus the locations of the diagonal corridors within the building – while appearing arbitrary – are actually the result of authentic human behavior. A wide number of student services were then placed along the routes to further increase pathway use.

Collaboration is essential to a project of this type. Early in the design process, Koolhaas and his firm OMA joined forces with the New York graphics firm 2 x 4 and Dutch designer Petra Blaisse with her firm Inside Outside. Together they created an arrangement of spaces that are a visual and kinesthetic delight. Elements of quiet amusement were brought to the building by 2 x 4's creation of monumental graphic images with textural patterns that, when approached, are discovered to be made up of innovative, small icons. They began by designing an international symbol for a solitary human and then further developed it to depict over two hundred human activities. The pictograms/icons were carefully arranged on the basis of their tonal value to correspond to the highlights and shadows of a photograph of Mies van der Rohe. As people approach the building a twenty-five-foot-high photographic portrait of Mies can be seen on the front doors; as they arrive at the automatic doors, however, they see the small activity icons that are etched onto the glass panels. Immediately within the Welcome Center people are greeted by seven huge portraits of the founders of IIT on the glass wall. Once again, as people approach for a closer examination, the small, round icons come into focus. Since the half-tone dots only register at a close distance – and the portraits from afar – it is amusing to watch people move back and forth as they attempt to "see" both aspects.

Pertra Blaisse and Inside Outside were responsible for the bold color scheme and three internal gardens. Inside, the 110,000-square-foot building becomes an internal landscape with a surprising number of ramps and stairs and natural sunlight streaming in. Flanking the sunken center court cafeteria are two "hills"; the outside, inaccessible Mies Garden, and the inside accessibility ramp intertwined with stairs. While the ramp is visually intriguing, it is dangerous as there are no railings along its sides and the use of the same color on the ramp and stair make it difficult to discern the stair tread edges.[3] Above the cafeteria and multi-tiered stair/ramp system are clerestory-like windows that provide a view of the hanging prairie grass gardens. This garden bridges over the cafeteria and ramp/stair, all of which are appropriately finished with a "sea-colored opalescent green that almost seems liquid" (Becker 2003: 25). The third internal patio garden has a large pine tree as its centerpiece and allows light to enter the office area.

Glossy epoxy-and-urethane poured flooring enhances the orange glow from the Panelite system throughout the building. In one area, a glowing crevice serves as the "Broadband" space where computers sit on an illuminated honeycomb counter. The flaming orange-red epoxy is used on the finish of the ramp, stairs, flooring and walls making it an extremely eye-catching space as our "attention is drawn instinctively to the brightest and most contrasting features of a scene" (Porter 1982: 49). Blaisse successfully uses the concept of "color detachment." Tom Porter describes this concept as occurring "when colour is used simply to celebrate architecture and intensify our experience of it; it is active rather than passive" (Porter 1982: 116). He explains that it "usually follows the designer's desire to create a new atmosphere with colour; a bright scheme tending to express architectural diversity, gaiety and excitement" (Porter 1982: 116). How appropriate – and compensatory – for a campus voted America's "least-beautiful" by college students in a 1997 national survey. Throughout the building the open spaces and glass walls make students highly visible, and even when not seen their voices travel throughout the building. One of the complex's ironies is that while great efforts were made to reduce the sound vibrations of the L, the real success is that the building vibrates with student life.

Notes

1. According to the "The McCormick Tribune Campus Center Fact Sheet" prepared by the Illinois Institute of Technology the passing commuter train noise is reduced by the tube from 120 decibels to approximately 70–80 decibels outside the building and to less than 70 decibels inside the building.
2. "A new era of architecture at IIT" http://masterplan.iit.edu/mccormick_gallery/summary.html. (accessed June 28, 2006).
3. While this terrain was meant as a student gathering area I have yet, during my numerous visits, to see anyone seated here. In fact, since opening, the stairs have been outlined with yellow tape and a long solid bench has been placed at the top stair to prevent people from accessing the stair from the central area. While visually unappealing they are both good ideas as some

of my students accidentally almost fell down the "terrain" before noticing the stairs.

References

Becker, L. 2003. "Of Mies and Rem." *Chicago Reader* (September 26), section 1.

Blackwell, E.C. 2004. *Frommer's Chicago 2004.* New York: Wiley Publishing, Inc.

Chicago Transit Authority and Lohan Associates. 1996. *Guidelines for Transit-Supporting Development*.

Porter, T. 1982. *Architectural Color*. New York: Whitney Library of Design.

Schafer, R.M. [1977] 1994. *The Soundscape: Our Sonic Environment and the Tuning of the World.* Rochester, VT: Destiny Books.

BOOK REVIEWS

The Senses and Aesthetics from a Scandinavian Perspective

Sense and Senses in Aesthetics, by Per Bäckström and Troels Degn Johansson (eds)

Göteborg, Sweden: NSU Press, 2003, 242 pages. ISBN 91-88484-24-6. 15 Euros

Larry Shiner

Larry Shiner is the author of *The Invention of Art: A Cultural History* (University of Chicago, 2001) and recently became Professor Emeritus of Philosophy at the University of Illinois at Springfield. lshin1@uis.edu

This anthology of essays by nine young Scandinavian scholars seeks to address a series of issues concerning the relation of sense to the senses, with the additional aim of giving the senses the kind of centrality in aesthetics hitherto held by the sign. Two crucial issues within this project are how to conceive of the relationship between art forms and the particular sense or senses appropriate to each art and how reflection on the senses will affect the idea of the unity of the arts. The essays fall rather neatly into two groups: four are general philosophical discussions of the relation of sense and the senses; the remaining five take up particular art forms or topics.

Of the essays devoted to specific arts, two deal with literature, two with film and one with food. Per Bäckström's piece, "Suspicion in the Ear: The Phonemic Reading of Garrett Stewart in a Scandinavian Context," deals with the relationship of eye and ear in the reading process, focusing on Stewart's emphasis on the inner sound of words. After a discussion of the connection between Stewart's idea of "transegmental drift" and Derrida's attack on phonocentrism, the author analyzes several Swedish poems in the light of Stewart's theory. The other literary essay, "In Rot Getaucht: Elias Canetti's *Die gerettete Zunge* and the Color 'Red' in Modern Art," by Karen Hvidfeldt Madsen discusses the symbolism of red in Canetti's autobiographical trilogy through an analysis of Canetti's reflections on his sensory development. There are also some interesting pages on Jewishness and red, Sylvia Plath's poetry and Krzysztof Kieslowski's film, *Trois Couleurs: Rouge*.

The two essays devoted entirely to film could not be more different from each other. Esben Krohn's "Prosthesis Unbound" devotes its opening pages to some general reflections on the nature of photography and film before focusing the remainder of the essay on several Danish silent films from the period 1910–13. The second film essay, "Holy Shit! Quentin Tarantino's Excremental Aesthetics" by Claus Krogholm Sand, is a meditation on the sacred and profane implications of violence and the metaphorical use of "shit" in Tarantino's *Pulp Fiction*. Sand seeks to rescue Tarantino's film from the charge of careless immorality.

Helle Brønnum Carlsen's "Taste as a matter of pedagogical concern" directly addresses gustatory taste and the question of food as an art form. Carlsen's main point about the symbolic nature of food draws heavily on Carolyn Korsmeyer's *Making Sense of Taste*, a dependence which Carlsen freely acknowledges. Her own contribution on the multiple facets of gustatory taste make this not only the most concrete essay in the anthology but probably most accessible to those interested in the bodily senses.

The four philosophical essays are largely expository, especially the three dealing with Jean-Luc Nancy, Michel Serres and Peter Sloterdijk. The fourth essay is largely an intellectual history of the use of the Orpheus myth from the German Romantics through Nietzsche to Maurice Blanchot. Mischa Sloth Carlsen's "Orpheus as Socrates Practicing Music: On the Synaesthetic Origin of Literary Philosophy," traces some interesting historical connections concerning the relation of the visual and the auditory in the Orpheus myth and its reappearance in the Romantic ideas of wit and irony. Unfortunately, the essay's prose is overwritten and full of lapidary assertions that detract from its genuine insights. The synesthesia of Carlsen's subtitle refers specifically to Nietzsche's attempt to unite the Apollonian (visual) and Dionysian (auditory) although the primary trajectory of her piece is to show how the Greek, Romantic and Nietzschean explorations eventuate in Blanchot's "orphic" literary theory.

Book Reviews

Many an anthology includes a piece or two that leaves the reader wondering what the connection is to the main theme. This is the case with Michael Penzold's otherwise useful "Challenging Modernism in Sloterdijk's Spheres," an exposition of the first two volumes of a projected trilogy by the German literary critic and philosopher Peter Sloterdijk. Written in an admirably clear prose, Penzold's essay attempts to explain Sloterdijk's rather vague notion of "spheres" as shared spaces of social and imaginative life. Although there is some talk about sights and sounds, the theme of the senses scarcely appears in direct form.

The two most consequential philosophical essays in the volume are those devoted to Nancy and Serres, both of whom have not only written extensively and explicitly on the theme of the senses, but also make tactility a central issue. As Erik Steinskog points out in his essay "Being Touched by Art: Art and Sense in Jean-Luc Nancy," Nancy sees touch as a paradigm of all the senses since it is a metaphor for feeling. Hence, he downplays literal tactility and speaks of touching at a distance, of touching with the eyes or the ear etc. The relevance of this for aesthetics, according to Nancy, derives from the way the work of art forces a sense to "touch itself," to be the sense that it is, to make a "world" out of sense. Steinskog also emphasizes Nancy's fascination with the semantic play of *sens* (sense) and *les sens* (senses) and its parallel in the idea of art and the arts. Steinskog's essay closes with some interesting reflections on touching both surface (skin) and the depth (soul/feelings) and how the work of art can touch us despite ourselves.

As Troels Degn Johansson emphasizes, touch is also the model sense for Michel Serres who speaks of a "general tactility" in *Les Cinq sens*. Although Serres also uses touch metaphorically, he tends to emphasize the physical reality of touch more than Nancy. Working from Lucretius's notion of images as membranes stripped from objects and hence literally touching us, Serres is led to the image of the world as a tissue. Our being-in-the-world is one of touching and being touched; sensation is a mingling of membranes. (In this respect he makes good use of St Veronica's shroud in evoking the tactility of the image.) Johansson pulls Serres's analysis toward aesthetics by focusing part of his essay on Serres's discussion of Pierre Bonnard's paintings. With Bonnard, Serres argues, the experience of painting is more tactile than visual. In Bonnard's nudes the skin is not "a vulgar object for the gaze, but a sensing subject" (p. 155). Johansson ends his essay by comparing Serres's ideas on the tactility of the image to some passages from Roland Barthes's *Camera Lucida* which also invoke Veronica's napkin and develop the idea that the photograph is literally an emanation of the referent.

There are two important limitations to this collection of essays. First, although the introductory editorial remarks acknowledge the important work on the senses done in the natural and social sciences, only one of the nine essays draws upon it. The second limitation is the exclusively continental focus of the more philosophical essays. Even so, there is much to learn from this anthology. If nothing else, it is a window on what counts as significant discourse on sense and the senses in the Scandinavian world.

A Sense of History

A History of the Senses: From Antiquity to Cyberspace, by Robert Jütte

Translated by James Lynn, Cambridge: Polity Press, 2005, 395 pages. PB 0-7456-2958-X. $26.95/£18.99.

Mark M. Smith

Mark M. Smith is Carolina Distinguished Professor of History at the University of South Carolina, Columbia, SC. His latest book is *How Race Is Made: Slavery, Segregation, and the Senses* (University of North Carolina Press). http://www.cas.sc.edu/hist/index.html

Choices can be a bit stark these days for avid readers of history. The standard, increasingly interior, academic monograph has recently been joined by two, often unsatisfying, types of book: the hefty tome devoted to a relatively and unreasonably small topic, its weight and size sometimes standing in for substance, and the self-consciously "epic" history erected on a spicy, chatty narrative that reads well but rarely asks readers to interrogate assumptions or think especially hard.

Then there's Robert Jütte's book, a wholly refreshing study that dares, in under four hundred pages, to tell a remarkably ambitious, intellectually sophisticated and lively story about the five senses from antiquity to the present.

Sensory history – or what Jütte sometimes refers to as the history of sense perception – is still in its infancy.

Fresh air for pedestrians; cartoon ("Old banger," 1904), from *Beiträge zur historischen Sozialkunde*, reproduced in Robert Jütte, *A History of the Senses*. The level of olfactory pollution suggested by this cartoon from 1904 leads Jütte to surmise that our sense of smell is no longer taking as much punishment as it once did.

According to Jütte, it "exists only in an incomplete state, with much of it consisting of individual historical treatments of the senses of sight, hearing, and smell" with studies of touch and taste especially thin on the ground (p. 13). He is quite right and has read enough in the secondary literature to know that what we need is a broad, historically and historiographically informed account detailing the history of the five senses. This, in essence, is what Jütte aims to give us and, for the most part, he succeeds admirably.

Jütte begins, quite properly, by stressing the need to historicize the senses. He makes the case that historians are under an obligation "to distinguish between the historicity of a physical experience (in this case, sense perception) and the form in which it has been preserved or handed down," that we "have to break with the aprioristic assumption of the 'naturalness' of sense perception," and correctly concludes that "there can be no such thing as a natural history of the senses, only a social history of sense perception" (pp. 8, 9). He then

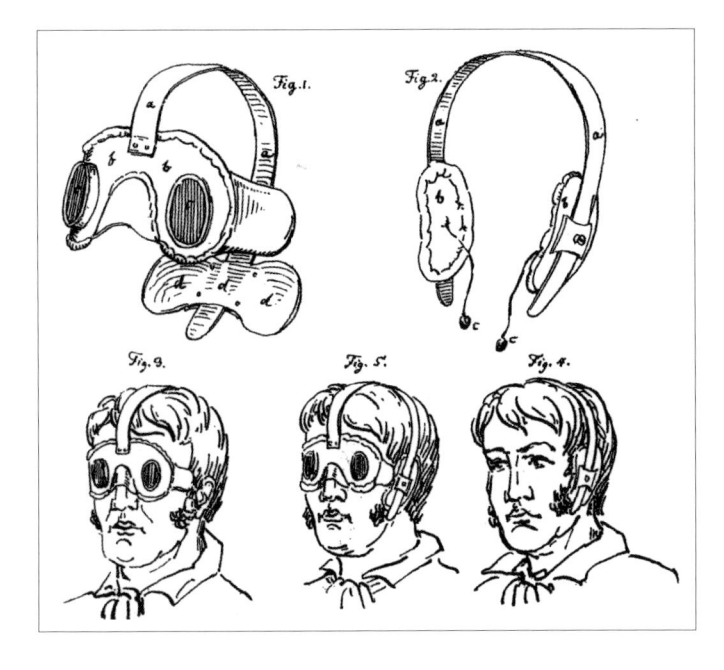

Plan for the isolation of vision and hearing proposed by the German author and doctor Ludwig Friedrich Froriep in 1846 as a cost-effective alternative to the solitary confinement cell. A further advantage, according to Froriep, was that "young criminals located in any part of the prison would be able to take part in communal religious and spiritual instruction with isolated eyes, and assemble for work and meals with isolated ears" (quotation and image both reproduced in Robert Jütte, *A History of the Senses*).

offers thoughtful treatments detailing the evolution of sensory imagery in literature, the relationship between the senses and medicine and the now familiar rise of vision and reason. In Jütte's telling, this is a story conveyed using largely literary and intellectual sources – Kant, Descartes, Locke and Hume, among others, come in for sustained analysis.

Throughout, Jütte's arguments are thoughtful, wide-ranging and erudite, demonstrating an impressive understanding of natural philosophy especially. He examines thinking on the senses from Plato to Kepler, and beyond, attending to how each conceived of the senses. Throughout, he tends to treat a given thinker's commentary on the senses as proxy for a broadly constituted statement on the significance and meaning of the senses for a given society. Because of his interest in the intellectual history of the senses, Jütte is especially good at tracing changes in the hierarchy of sensory ideas over time and he concludes that the "traditional division of the senses into those that were more mental (seeing and hearing) and those that were more physical (taste, smell and touch) retained its validity until well into the modern era" (p.52).

Different evidence would temper this argument, however, and it is worth pointing out that although Jütte does attend to the history of the senses in some non-Western societies, most obviously in his fascinating discussion of Indian and Chinese natural philosophy, his evidentiary basis is not only very Western but quite German at that. Moreover, Jütte often presents powerful evidence that suggests that some key Enlightenment thinkers were not as resolutely visualist as we have sometimes been led to believe. Such evidence could – and, according to Jessica Riskin's impressive recent study, perhaps should – urge scholars to question more closely the often assumed intimacy between Enlightenment, sight and reason. Much more could be made of this but Jütte, despite the impressive quality of his own evidence, tends to leave unchallenged the common wisdom and perpetuates the association of the Enlightenment with vision, reason, and truth.

In other words, Jütte's epistemology tends to work, even if unwittingly, within the coordinates of the great divide theory, an interpretation that stresses how the revolution in print and the imperatives of the Enlightenment, in his words, ushered in the "reign of the eye and the sense of vision," which "continues to this day" and denigrated the other senses (pp.15–16). This observation is confusing not least because a good deal of Jütte's excellent book shows how very important nonvisual senses were to the rise of modernity. He provides dozens of examples attesting to the relevance of, for example, smell, noise, taste and touch to urbanization and industrialization. Jütte's closing chapters, which claim to demonstrate "a strange renaissance" in things sensate, a "rediscovery" of the senses thanks to commercialization, the internet and, especially, "the growing needs of a post-industrial leisure society" (p.16) are, given the evidence he presents showing the continued relevance of all the senses in the modern period generally, rather puzzling. A more flexible theoretical framework, one less indebted to the great divide or orality theory, would have helped Jütte explain more fully the historical significance of the continued relevance of nonvisual senses under modernity. As it stands, that importance is certainly apparent from Jütte's book but we have no clear explanation of why nonvisual senses not only remained relevant to the project of modernity but, in fact, often seemed so central to its creation.

All things considered, Robert Jütte has given us a book of signal import. Anyone working on the history of the senses simply must consult it. It is not the last word on the topic – and Jütte nowhere claims it will be – but it is a landmark study in the history of the senses and anyone hoping to write a sensory history will read this impressive book with profit.

References

Riskin, Jessica. 2002. *Science in the Age of Sensibility: The Sentimental Empiricists of the French Enlightenment*. Chicago: University of Chicago Press.

On the Varieties of Experience

Songs of Experience: Modern American and European Variations on a Universal Theme, by Martin Jay

Berkeley: University of California Press, 2005, 431 pages. PB 0-520-24823-6, $21.95/£13.95.

C. Jason Throop

C. Jason Throop is an assistant professor of anthropology at the University of California, Los Angeles.
jthroop@ucla.edu

With this book Martin Jay provides us with an elegantly written, vastly comprehensive and carefully researched account of the intellectual history of the meaning of the concept of experience in modern North American and European thought. This is no easy task given what Jay reveals to be the inherently polysemic and ambiguous nature of the term. Indeed, some may believe in light of this ambiguity that Alfred North Whitehead (1927) was right when he said that the "word 'experience' is the most deceitful in philosophy." What supporters of Whitehead's assessment may see as a fundamental weakness in the use of a term that regularly resists definitional clarity, precision and rigor Jay takes to be at the heart of the very challenge and virtue of pursuing the history of the idea in modern philosophical thought.

Freeing himself from the project of seeking to determine a singular or authentic referent for the concept, Jay sets out instead to investigate experience's varied and often contradictory meanings. In fact, the very richness of the term's multiple significations underpins Jay's decision to employ William Blake's pluralized metaphor of "songs of experience" for the book's title. With a reference to auditory experience in the book's title, readers of this journal who are also familiar with Jay's book *Downcast Eyes: The Denigration of Vision in Twentieth-Century French Thought* (1993) will not be surprised to discover that many of the varied meanings of experience are rooted in the sensory, a theme that is clearly discussed throughout the book. For instance, Jay illustrates how Bacon's and Descartes's reliance upon vision as a distal sensory modality became implicated in generating objective and reliable forms of knowledge (Chapter One), he examines empiricist understandings of experience through presenting the debate of Locke and Berkeley over primary and secondary qualities (Chapter Two), and he investigates the place of taste and judgment in the perception and evaluation of aesthetic objects (Chapter Four). That said, readers should also be forewarned that an explicit focus on sensation is much muted by comparison with his previous work.

According to Jay, what allows experience to hold within its semantic grasp such multiple understandings is precisely what he observes to be a paradoxical tension in a word that is, on the one hand, a linguistic signifier with a complex collective conceptual history that ties together various "heterogeneous signifieds." While it is, on the other hand, an almost poetic reminder "that such concepts always leave a remainder that escapes their homogenizing grasp" (p. 6). Indeed, the term "experience" seems to straddle a space between the publicly accessible realm of communicative forms and the necessarily deferred private realm of subjective life. Simultaneously evoking expressive commonalities and ineffable interiorities, the concept of experience thus encompasses a rather broad, and at times contradictory, range of denotations. In an attempt to deal with this complexity, Jay organizes the book into chapters that set out to detail various modalities of experience – including, epistemological (Chapter Two), religious (Chapter Three), aesthetic (Chapter Four), political (Chapter Five) and historical (Chapter Six) – and key approaches to the topic in the history of philosophy and social theory – for example, classical, enlightenment and romantic (Chapter One), empiricist and idealist (Chapter Two), pragmatic (Chapter Seven), critical (Chapter Eight) and poststructuralist (Chapter Nine).

Despite the heterogeneity of experience's arch of significations, early in the book Jay provides an etymological examination of the term that elicits a number of core sedimented meanings, among them: (a) a link to direct, raw and unreflective sensation or unmediated observation; (b) a privileging of the particular over the general or universal; and (c) an encompassing of a basic distinction between passivity and activity. Moreover, bearing down on the German terms *Erlebnis* and *Erfahrung* – two terms that are evoked repeatedly throughout the book – Jay teases out two basic contrasting understandings of the concept that are not directly evident in the single English term. As he explains, where *Erlebnis* generally refers to a view of experience as pre-objective, pre-reflective, immediate, momentary, undifferentiated and personal, *Erfahrung* tends to be associated with "a more temporally elongated notion of experience based on a learning process, an integration of discrete moments of experience into a narrative whole or an adventure" (11). Whereas the former is based primarily in sensory, perceptual, lived and embodied processes, the latter is more often rooted in narratively configured, cognitive, evaluative, mnemonic and expressive forms.

Jay is masterful in weaving a complex narrative that covers in impressive detail the work of thinkers ranging from Aristotle to Montaigne to James to Adorno to Foucault. Despite the diversity of approaches to understanding experience in the work of these various scholars, Jay identifies six main themes that provide discernable interlocking threads that are woven throughout the work. First, there is a recurrent interest in the relationship between a holistic understanding of experience as a unifying and all-encompassing category and a view of experience in terms of distinctive modes.

Second, Jay returns in various contexts to discuss numerous debates held between differing philosophers and social theorists over possible existing relationships between the experiencing subject and the object of experience. As Jay reveals, such debates tend to revolve around such questions as: Do varieties of experience exist in which there are no longer epistemological or phenomenological distinctions between subject and object (for instance William James's notion of "pure experience")? If so, what is the relationship between such non-dualistic modes of experience and those varieties of experience in which distinctions between subject and object are more clearly marked?

A third theme is tied to differing views on how to understand the relationship between experience and language. The questions most often highlighted by Jay here include: Is experience merely a product of language and discursive forms? Are there forms of experience that are somehow "non-linguistic" or "non-discursive"? Do embodied and sensory forms of experience necessarily entail a form of immediacy that outstrips linguistic frames of understanding? Are narrative formulation, forms of Freudian secondary elaboration and/or retrospective assessment the primary or exclusive means through which authentic varieties of experience are articulated? And, if so, are there forms of experience (e.g. Bataille's and Foucault's notion of "limit experiences," James's and Otto's understanding of mystical experience, Benjamin's view of traumatic experience etc.) that resist or inform such points of articulation?

Fourth, in various chapters of the book, there is a return to examining questions bearing on how it is that we should go about understanding the relative activity or passivity of experience. In other words, is experience something that is necessarily constituted by an active, intentional subjectivity or is it something that is primarily passively undergone, endured and suffered through? Is an *a priori*, Kantian-inspired subjective constructivism or an empiricist, *a posteriori* passive acquiescence to external conditions a more accurate account of the true nature of experience? Alternatively, is it possible to imagine a perspective in which active and passive renderings of experience are understood to coexist, as in the case of what William James termed the "double barreled" nature of experience?

Fifth, there is a recurring theme that is tied to questioning the extent to which experience should be viewed as associated with the interiority, the privacy and the putatively deeply personal realm of the subject. If experience is primarily subjective, are there ways in which experience can be effectively shared with others? More specifically, are there mutually intelligible forms of experience that can be translated across historical periods and cultural boundaries (a perspective inherent in Wilhelm Dilthey's notion of "re-experiencing," R.G. Collingwood's notion of "re-enactment" and E.P. Thompson's view of developing a "history from below")? Or is experience so diverse that translation is rendered extremely difficult if not impossible between individuals inhabiting differing subject positions, classes, ethnicities, cultures or historical periods (a view held by the historian Joan Scott and the historian of anthropology James Clifford, among others)?

Finally, sixth, throughout the book discourses of experience re-emerge that lament the loss of "authentic experience." Whether this investment in reclaiming "authentic experience" is understood in terms of resistance to the epistemological reduction of experience to its cognitive forms, the commodification of experience in capitalist and post-capitalist societies, the alienation of individuals from "holistic" experience in modern life or the atrophying of agency in the face of political oppression, ever diffusing regimes of power or outright violence, experience when conceived as "authentic" seems to imply a beyond, or a something more than is encapsulated in such reductionistic frames. With thinkers as diverse as Michel de Montaigne, William James, John Dewey, Raymond Williams, George Bataille, Walter Benjamin, Michel Foucault and Theodor Adorno we see, however, a similar critique of "overly claimed" varieties of experience that are held to stifle the possibility inherent in "authentic" experience for indeterminacy, openness, change and flux.

In terms of the book's very few inadequacies there is only one that is worth noting here. As Jay himself acknowledges in the Introduction, any history of a concept as prevalent and polysemous as experience will necessarily be a partial account; one that will significantly evidence the historian's own interests, competencies and particularly their point of entry into the problem at hand (for instance the chapter devoted to Benjamin and Adorno is clearly reflective of Jay's early acquaintance with, and mastery of, the Frankfurt school). For this reason, there will inevitably be readers who will take issue with Jay's points of emphasis and his decisions regarding the inclusion or exclusion of particular thinkers or traditions. That said, given the prominent and influential role that phenomenology and existentialism have played throughout modern articulations of the concept of experience in both Europe and America, I believe that this book would have greatly benefited from the inclusion of an independent chapter outlining the significant contributions and critiques of this tradition. Also, as an anthropologist invested in examining the history of theories of experience in the discipline (cf. Throop 2003, 2005), I cannot help but find Jay's very brief reference to the work of Victor Turner, Edward Bruner and Barbara Myerhoff to be rather unsatisfying. These rather minor critiques aside I cannot stress enough the importance and impressive scope of this book. It is a book that will significantly contribute not only to social theory and philosophy broadly defined but also, even despite its relatively muted engagement with sensation *per se*, to ongoing attempts in the pages of this journal and elsewhere to achieve better understanding of how, historically, the senses and various forms of sensation have been and continue to be implicated in differing registers of experience in modern Western thought.

References

Jay, Martin. 1993. *Downcast Eyes: The Denigration of Vision in Twentieth-Century French Thought.* Berkeley: University of California Press.

Throop, C. Jason. 2003. "Articulating Experience." *Anthropological Theory*, 3(2): 219–241.

——. 2005. "Hypocognition, a 'Sense of the Uncanny, and the Anthropology of Ambiguity: Reflections on Robert I. Levy's Contribution to Theories of 'Experience' in Anthropology." *Ethos*, 33(4): 499–511.

Whitehead, Alfred North. 1927. *Symbolism: Its Meaning and Effect.* New York: Macmillan.

Sign up for Contents Alerting Now! http://bod.sagepub.com

Body & Society

Published in association with TCS

Editors **Mike Featherstone** Nottingham Trent University, UK and **Bryan S Turner** National University of Singapore

"**Body & Society** promises an exciting and informed critique of our contemporary patterns of body behaviour." **Times Higher Education Supplement**

Body & Society is a companion journal to **Theory, Culture & Society**, launched to cater for the upsurge of interest in the social and cultural analysis of the human body that has taken place in recent years.

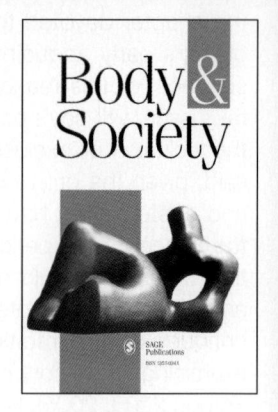

Body & Society follows the philosophy of **Theory, Culture & Society** in terms of its theoretical openness, critical exploration of existing traditions, and commitment to the analysis of a diverse range of themes. It encourages inter- and transdisciplinary foci and is particularly concerned to feature innovative analyses.

The journal is dedicated to the publication of contemporary empirical and theoretical work from a wide range of disciplines, including anthropology, art history, communications, cultural history, cultural studies, feminism, film studies, health studies, leisure studies, medical history, philosophy, psychology, religious studies, sociology and sports studies.

Body & Society centrally concerns itself with debates in feminism, technology, ecology, postmodernism, medicine, ethics and consumerism which take the body as the central analytic issue in the questioning of established paradigms.

The journal examines the extensive range of issues that have emerged from these debates by engaging with the contributions of writers such as:

- Baudrillard • Bourdieu • Butler • Cixous • Douglas • Elias • Foucault
- Haraway • Kristeva • Mauss • Merleau-Ponty • Schilder

Free online sample copy available!
http://bod.sagepub.com

Quarterly: March, June, September, December
ISSN: 1357-034X

Subscription Hotline +44 (0)20 7324 8701 **Email** subscription@sagepub.co.uk

$SAGE Publications
www.sagepublications.com

EXHIBITION REVIEWS

Sonambiente Berlin 2006
Festivale für hören und sehen

Akademie der Künste and other locations, Berlin, June 1–July 16, 2006

Rosemary Heather

Rosemary Heather is the editor of *C Magazine*, a visual arts quarterly published in Toronto. She is also the curator of the exhibitions I Beg to Differ (London, 1996) and Serial Killers: Elements of Painting Multiplied X Six Artists (Toronto/London, 2000).
rosemheather@yahoo.ca

Shown at a number of locations in Berlin, *Sonambiente: Festivale für hören und sehen* ("Festival of Hearing and Seeing") took place within the wider context of the 2006 World Cup. This was a circumstance that found its most tangible expression at the Brandenbrug Gate branch of the Akademie der Künst. Situated next to the Gate, on the Pariser Platz, the Akademie also happened to be at the start of the so-called fan mile. Running along the tree-lined boulevard that connects the Gate to the city's Victory Column, on bleachers temporarily erected for the occasion, audiences of up to 700,000 people congregated the length of the fan mile to watch live football broadcasts on giant TV screens.

Two basic assumptions framed the event. The first was that sound art is somehow intrinsically populist. Acknowledging that it sat at the doorstep of an uncommonly powerful global event, the Akademie offered fans the "Public Viewing World Cup Sound Art Lounge," which bracketed screenings of each game with various sound art events, most of them themed DJ evenings. Presumably the idea was to offer fans a gateway to the appreciation of other types of sound-based phenomena. The second, more interesting, premise was that the festival would in effect provide the context to enable an experience of the city of Berlin as "an actual work of sound art." By stating its desire to make a connection between "urban experience and sound experience," the festival organizers revealed a preference for cultural sounds, as opposed to those found in nature – if one could put it like that. It was a distinction made if only for the purposes of shedding light on a deeper bias: that is, in favor of the synthetic character of urban sound experience and its innate connection to spectacle.

The idea that sound-based art may lead on to thoughts about spectacle proves useful when considering the artworks presented by the event. It suggests criteria for evaluating the work that is otherwise lacking in the catchall category of sound art. This is especially true because, as a mode of art making that is about aural experience but is not music, sound art has long operated as a subgenre of modernist art practice. Dedicated to experimentation with volume and the spatial, durational and physical effects of sound, it falls within the larger modernist project of finding ways to give tangible expression to a medium's formal properties.

Much of the work presented by Sonambiente adhered to this modernist formula. Austrian artist Bernard Leitner's *Kaskade* (2006), a sound installation in a kidney-shaped stairwell, provided one of the more stellar examples of this type of practice. Six tweeter-fitted parabolic bowls mounted in the twelve-story stairwell created cascading effects of sound that changed according to where one was standing. As with the best of these types of experiments, the

Figure 1
Bernard Leitner, *Kaskade* (2006), sound installation. Photograph by Kay-Uwe Rosseburg, courtesy of Sonambiente Berlin 2006.

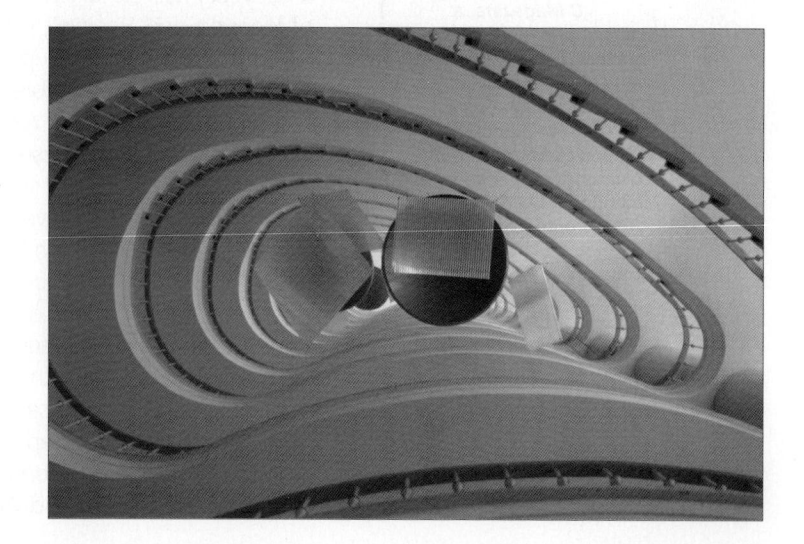

Exhibition Reviews

Figure 2 (a), (b)
Kris Vleeschouwer, *Glassworks, a+b* (2005), interactive sound installation. Photograph © Carine De Meter, courtesy of Sonambiente Berlin 2006.

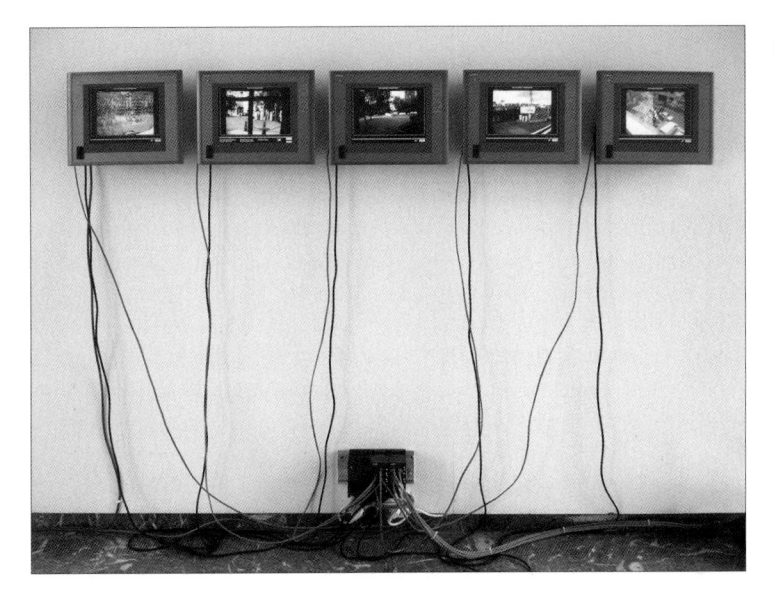

Exhibition Reviews

aural effects had tangible physical and almost visible correlates to create a physically embodied experience of the architectural space.

Belgian artist Kris Vleeschouwer's *Glassworks, a+b* (2005), consisted of 10,000 glass bottles sitting on a mechanized industrial shelving unit. Connected by an ADSL line to five glass-recycling containers around Berlin, the shelving moved every time someone threw a bottle away, displacing the bottles in the gallery so that they smashed to the floor. Although breaking glass always brings with it some residual excitement, the work never quite escaped the banality of its conceptual framework: people recycle and accidents happen, whether causally connected or incidental, both are unremarkable occurrences in everyday life.

The disjunction in timeframes that are always a part of the historical condition was addressed by *Opera for a Small Room* (2005) by the Canadians Janet Cardiff and George Bures Miller.

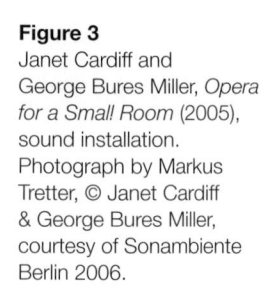

Figure 3
Janet Cardiff and George Bures Miller, *Opera for a Small Room* (2005), sound installation. Photograph by Markus Tretter, © Janet Cardiff & George Bures Miller, courtesy of Sonambiente Berlin 2006.

Viewers looked through the windows of a cabin built to scale in an interior filled from top to bottom with old fashioned record players, twenty-four antique speakers and almost 2,000 long-playing record albums. Over the course of twenty minutes a scenario played out. Animatronic activation of the record players, and light and audio elements evoked a tale about an opera-obsessed individual who retreated to this cabin to play music and reflect on his life. A voice distorted as if speaking through a megaphone and dreamy as if lost in thought, provided the basic elements of a narrative. Orchestral and pop music, arias from operas and ambient sound effects such as the thunderous noise from a passing train were layered together to create a fully immersive art experience. So persuasive was the mise-en-scène of this work that the one had to stop and remind oneself that what one was watching was happening but not actually there; no one sat in this cabin playing records. Existing in the imagination in some melancholy Canadian backwoods, far from the urban milieu that creates opera and even history, the work sat, in fact, in an art gallery in Berlin. The Sonambiente festival provided no better example of our susceptibility to the seductions of virtual experience. Perhaps it was the work's dislocation of locales and implied historical timeframes (record albums are a thing of the past) that helped to make tangible the synthetic nature of the world it created. The artists had no need to avail themselves of futuristic metaphors to make visible the fantastic virtual character of the reality that comprises much of contemporary experience. Instead they made use of a slight historical time lag to give sharp focus onto the world of the present. What made this work most relevant to the spectacle of the World Cup occurring all around it was the awareness it created of how the form rather than the content of an experience enables its expression. In discussing such a large and varied event as Sonambiente 2006 it might seem odd to say that one work more than all the others fully met the event's ambitions to provide a critical context for a sports event with an unprecedented media reach, but this would only be to point out just how elusive critical reflection on the present can be.

PORTALS
Opening Doorways to Other Realities Through the Senses

by Lynne Hume

'Magic, mystery, madness and meaning are all tackled in Lynne Hume's brilliant, wide ranging discussion that opens doorways to richer understanding of the ways in which people access other realities.'

Graham Harvey, Lecturer in Religious Studies, The Open University

As Alice discovered in Wonderland, cave entrances, tunnels, spirals and mirrors can transport people to strange worlds where anything is possible. *Portals* investigates how we move beyond the conscious and physical world using our senses, into other realities of the spiritual and the divine.

December 2006 • 224pp
ISBN 978 1 84520 145 6 (PB) £19.99 • $34.95
ISBN 978 1 84520 144 9 (HB) £55.00 • $99.95
www.bergpublishers.com

BERG

Arsenal
Artists Exploring the Potential of Sound as a Weapon

Alma Enterprises, London, June 23–August 6, guest curated by Ellen Mara De Wachter.

Francis Summers

Francis Summers, Critical Theory Lecturer at the University College for the Creative Arts at Rochester (UK), is a practicing artist. He has exhibited at the Centro Cultural Telemar, Rio de Janeiro, Brazil and the Rotterdam Foto-Biennial, Holland. He is currently researching a Ph.D. by practice at the Royal College of Art, London, on enjoyment and appropriation art. francis_summers@talk21.com

The use of sound as a weapon was largely brought to the fore in 1989 when the US restructuring of Panama's government in Operation Just Cause culminated in deafening loud pop music being played around the clock at a besieged General Manuel Noriega. These tactics, having been proved successful, have since been repeated, most notably during the FBI siege of David Koresh and his followers in Waco, Texas, when apparently the sounds of rabbits being slaughtered were used as part of the sonic assault. Sensorial assault has also become an integral part of interrogation techniques in the current war on terror, it being reported that theme tunes from children's television, including the cuddly dinosaur show *Barney*, are played repeatedly to break down detainee resistance.

In this ever-expanding context of aural violence perpetrated by different organizations in, or of, power *Arsenal: Artists Exploring the Potential of Sound as a Weapon* attempts to recoup "sonic weaponry" within a resistant artist–activist position. Taking place at Alma Enterprises, an artist-run gallery space in London's East End under the direction of the LAND cooperative, and curated by Ellen Mara De Wachter, it brings together a number of related practices that aim to take account of various uses of sound and/as violence. With its title one might expect an all-out sonic assault, yet what one encounters is a fairly cerebral and engaging affair that seeks to encompass its audience in a sustained dialogue rather than drive them screaming from the kind of barrages that provide the inception of the show.

The works in Arsenal engage directly with a number of real-time, real-world events fusing direct action with gallery experience. An example of this foray into the muddy waters of the political sphere is Thomas Altheimer's *Impossible. And yet there it is! No, impossible. Parallel Action # 3.3.048 – A Sonic Attack on Guantanamo Bay* (2006). This video documentation of his performance revolves around his broadcasting Beethoven's *Eroica* on a feebly small stereo towards the infamous Camp Delta dressed in a suit as his alter-ego "Thomas Herzon." Often posing bathetically as the European fool alongside the local help, the Herzon-figure's failed escapades addresses a wider question of possible agency in current political activism and the searching of the middle-class for identity in revolt. Admitting his own impotence in the face of the real-time situation, Altheimer's piece is a parody of self-betterment over productive social change. In a parallel vein, Rod Dickinson's *Nocturn: The Waco Re-enactment, September 16 2004* (2006) is a video documentation of a performance event the artist organized, reconstructing psychotronic aspects from the siege at Waco. The video of the event shows the audience turning up at London's Institute for Contemporary Art one evening to be met by stern quasi-military guards who deliver them via coaches to an unnamed stadium. Initially divided into gendered groups and aggressively made to sign disclaimer forms, the mood of the transported audience seems to shift from playful expectation to berated confusion. When they have been delivered into the stadium the video demonstrates some of the stimuli that were unleashed including bright lights, interminable broadcasts of beeping phones, slowed-down voices and extracts from telephone interviews between Koresh and the FBI agents. The piece produces a narrative of collapsed expectation and the sensorial aspects of siege warfare while avoiding a moralistic tone in favor of an affective reconstruction of the events.

More abstract works in the show include Pablo Gav's *Music Pissing on Flies Shitting on Bombs* (2006); described by the artist in the show's catalog as a "discrete, peaceful and yet aggressive emotional prelude" (2006: 39) this is an intermittently hissing musical composition that welcomes one at the gallery's doorstep. Tillman Terbuyken and Thomas Baldischwyler's humorous *Untitled* (2006) is a sculpture comprised of a painted, wall-mounted canvas drum softly emitting a Glenn Gould rendition of Bach and a carpet that triggers

Exhibition Reviews

Figure 1 (a), (b), (c)
Rod Dickinson, *Nocturn: The Waco Re-enactment, September 16 2004* (2006), still from DVD. Photographs by courtesy of the artist and LAND.

Exhibition Reviews

Figure 2
allsopp&weir, *To the Place or Being in the Place* (2006), still from DVD. Photograph by courtesy of the artists and LAND.

an ear-splitting barrage of noise when stood on. Placed in front of the painted drum, the carpet prevents any intimate engagement with the instrument's faintly embedded visual component, forcing a choice between an oblique approach and a direct plunge into an aural abyss. Treading another line between the intelligibile and the incomprehensible is allsopp&weir's *To the Place or Being in the Place* (2006), a video projection of overgrown urban spaces accompanied by two sound tracks. The almost-pastoral scenes of courtyards overgrown with ivy serve as a ground for a figurative movement of two voices. The first, broadcast into the gallery space, is a crisp English voice briskly narrating set phrases from language tapes. The other, heard through headphones, is the stumbling voice of a non-native English speaker attempting to keep up with the onrushing words. Lists such as "here we are/here's the hotel/here's your ice-cream" or "that's my husband/that's my mother/that's my sister" are spoken and fail to be spoken at the same time. The emotive impact of the work is that it demonstrates an inherent violence within language and symbolic networks of meaning. The gold standard of correct form is put forward as an ideal against which the contingent user is judged and punished. As an audience member one is put in a tentative space of identification and misrecognition, witnessing a painful aural mirror-stage with all the attendant vicissitudes of narcissism and aggression. The stumbling substance of the voice produces a certain remainder, of both pleasure and pain, that haunts the concepts of ownership and mastery that the phrases "that's your/that's my..." point towards.

The accompanying exhibition catalog collects together a number of essays, participating artist statements and textual documentations of many of the works. While some elements of this exhibition are in danger of falling short of delivering their message with full clarity the catalog ties together many of the threads that are left dangling, giving another welcome dimension Especially interesting is Steve Goodman's essay, entitled "Sonic Warfare: The Logistics of Affection," which informatively broadens the historical scope of the show by listing the mobilizations of the acoustic in the name of the so-called military–industrial complex. Ranging in scope from political organization to the edges of experimentation his examples include the importance of the loudspeaker in the Third Reich and Vladimir Gavreau's infrasonic bombardment of internal organs in the 1960s. More contemporary examples cited are the development of the Mosquito, a high-frequency sound device designed to target loitering teenagers, and the Israeli Army's uses of sound-cannons against Palestinian rioters. A gloomy Orwellian vision is brewed up here, combined with a certain gleeful and infectious Deleuzian hyperbole, as when Goodman calls on artists and musicians to develop an understanding of "viral infiltration, affective contagion, and cultural distribution of the war machine into the quotidian foldings of the sonic body, its sensations, rhythms and desires" (2006: 13). In this text, as well as in the exhibition space, post-structuralism, information theory and cultural resistance become fused in a nebulous zone, asking the audience to consider critically events where bodies, noises and powers collide.

References
Gav, Pablo. 2006. "Music Pissing on Flies Shitting on Bombs." In Ellen Mara De Wachter (ed.), *Arsenal: Artists Exploring the Potential of Sound as a Weapon*. London: Alma Enterprises.

Goodman, Steve. 2006. "Sonic Warfare: The Logistics of Affection." In Ellen Mara De Wachter (ed.), *Arsenal: Artists Exploring the Potential of Sound as a Weapon*. London: Alma Enterprises.

PARKETT

A SMALL MUSEUM AND A LARGE LIBRARY WITH CONTEMPORARY ARTISTS

For further information on subscriptions,
back issues and editions, please contact:

PARKETT · QUELLENSTRASSE 27 · 8031 ZÜRICH
TELEFON +41-44-271 81 40 · FAX +41-44-272 43 01

PARKETT · 145 AV. OF THE AMERICAS · N.Y. 10013
PHONE 212 - 673 2660 · FAX 212 - 271 0704

WWW.PARKETTART.COM